...VELOPMENT SERIES

General Editors: David Hopkins...

LEARNING SCHOOLS, LEARNING SYSTEMS

OTHER TITLES IN THE SCHOOL DEVELOPMENT SERIES:

M. Barber with R. Dann:
Raising Education Standards in the Inner Cities

R. Bollington, D. Hopkins and M. West:
An Introduction to Teacher Appraisal

Judith Chapman, William Boyd, Rolf Lander and David Reynolds:
The Reconstruction of Education

J. Chapman, Vern Wilkinson and D. Aspin:
Quality Schooling

P. Dalin:
School Development

P. Dalin:
How Schools Improve

P. Dalin and V. Rust:
Towards Schooling for the Twenty-first Century

P. Dalin with H.-G. Rolff:
Changing the School Culture

M. Fullan:
The New Meaning of Educational Change

D. Hargreaves and D. Hopkins:
The Empowered School

D. Hopkins, M. Ainscow and M. West:
School Improvement in an Era of Change

D. Hopkins and D. Hargreaves:
Development Planning for School Improvement

K. S. Louis and M. B. Miles:
Improving the Urban High School

J. Murphy:
Restructuring Schools

D. Reynolds and P. Cuttance:
School Effectiveness

P. Ribbins and E. Burridge:
Improving Education

J. Scheerens:
Effective Schooling

H. Silver:
Good Schools, Effective Schools

C. Taylor Fitz-Gibbon:
Monitoring Education

M. Wallace and A. McMahon:
Planning for Change in Turbulent Times

LEARNING SCHOOLS, LEARNING SYSTEMS

Paul Clarke

CONTINUUM

London and New York

To Eithne, Alice, Imogen, Isaac and Hannah

Continuum

Wellington House   370 Lexington Avenue
125 Strand   New York
London WC2R 0BB   NY 10017-6503

First published 2000

British Library Cataloguing-in-Publication Data
A catalogue record for this book is available from the British Library.

ISBN 0–8264–4804–6 (hardback)
     0–8264–4800–3 (paperback)

Excerpt from 'Little Gidding' in *Collected Poems 1919–1962* by T.S. Eliot, copyright 1936 by Harcourt, Inc., copyright © 1964, 1963 by T.S. Eliot, reprinted by permission of the publishers, Harcourt, Inc., Orlando, Florida, and Faber and Faber Ltd, London (see p. 144).

Typeset by York House Typographic Ltd, London
Printed and bound in Great Britain by Redwood Books, Trowbridge, Wiltshire

Contents

Series Editors' Foreword

Education in most advanced industrial societies has become more and more a 'managed' system. Targets are set, improvement documents written, teaching and schooling methods are legislated for and performance is measured and rewarded, or punished. The managerial practices of sectors such as commerce and industry are increasingly regarded as appropriate for the very different domain of education.

This is an important book that sets out another vision to replace managerialism – a vision of a learning school in which educational professionals improve their schools creatively, and therefore their learners, adopting principles of collaboration, risking, questioning, adaptivity, transformation, holistic thinking and wholeness, with the entire process seen as a learning journey.

But the book is not just an outline of a new way of thinking about educational change; it is a practical manual of what have been the experiences of schools that have embarked upon this new journey that Paul Clarke supports, and the lessons they have learned. Using detailed evidence derived from his work as a consultant with schools, the author outlines a new model whereby schools move beyond the seeking of false certainties towards a new model of school improvement in which data is used to identify problems, chart solutions and steer new courses. In the new model of school improvement, schools are encouraged to 'dig deeper' into themselves as organizations, and the staff are encouraged to 'dig deeper' to analyse their own needs and possible educational goals. The argument is that in a complex world, complex formulations of schools and complexity in the educational worlds of those that staff them are the only way to develop learning organizations that have the capacity to respond to societal change that itself is becoming ever more rapid, global and potentially disruptive.

For those of us in the disciplines of school effectiveness and school improvement, there is so much to take note of. Whether we wished it to or not, our work has been used to support managerially orientated policies within many countries. The original, radical commitment of school effectiveness to a mission that placed children's learning at its heart, and of school improvement to a self-reviewing school, as well as a self-managing one, may have been de-emphasized in the process.

Paul Clarke wants us to celebrate, design and implement different visions – of empowerment, of creative possibilities, of challenging and contesting the status quo, and of people who believe in each other's potential. We are very pleased indeed that this stimulating yet practical book is in the series, and hope sincerely that it will challenge those of us who need to be challenged and support those of us who are already working on the task of creating learning schools.

David Hopkins
David Reynolds

Acknowledgements

Warm and sincere thanks to those people who have helped: to David Hopkins and David Reynolds for their unstinting encouragement to keep on going at it; to Mel Ainscow for his bracing and loving advice on the wild first draft; to Mel West for pointing out the obvious when it wasn't obvious to me; to Louise Stoll and Kate Myers for guiding me to find my own voice. To Jane Reed, whose clarity and sensitivity made sure I attended to what I felt mattered. To Harold Williams, Maurice Smith and Peter Greenhalg for the many conversations we have had as the work has evolved and for letting me loose in so many schools to try things out. To Marie and Mike Boyd-Clarke and Sharon Shoesmith for the insights and analysis. To Tom Christie for helping me take the formative steps. To the staff at Continuum, particularly Anthony Haynes, Alan Worth and Mandy MacDonald. To Tony Townsend for vision and internationalism. To Erik Knudsen, my film-maker friend, for the many evenings of insightful and illuminating discussion 'transcending the immediate and capturing the essence of the new'. To **The wineplace.com** and Chris, Marshy and Chris for keeping me on the rails. To Coventry City for teaching me that it is OK to continue to struggle; to the Lake District for being there. To my dad Gerry, whose endless willingness to talk it over enabled me to keep going when I felt like giving in, to my mum Heather for sorting out the kids over the summer so I could write, and to Eithne for making me see the funny side, even when I lost a chapter in the machine, and for putting up with my preoccupations. Finally, to my beautiful children Alice, Imogen, Isaac and Hannah, who motivate and inspire me with their exhausting and effortless appetite for learning and for loving life.

Here is Edward Bear, coming downstairs, now, bump, bump, bump on the back of his head behind Christopher Robin.

It is, as far as he knows, the only way of coming downstairs, but sometimes he feels that there really is another way, if only he could stop for a moment and think of it.

A. A. Milne, *Winnie the Pooh*

Preface

My intention is to tell
Of bodies changed to different forms . . .
The heavens and all below them, Earth and her creatures,
All change, and we, part of creation,
Also must suffer change.

Ovid, *Metamorphoses*

I have just returned from a family holiday in Cornwall. A little village that we visited holds a festival each year to celebrate a local legend about an evil black sea dragon and the power residing in the light of ships' lanterns. It is a convoluted story, ending with the dragon captured inside a ring of light which sees his demise. During the day of the festival the people of the town, and any others who care to join in, get together and a small stage is erected, musicians come and go, singing and dancing takes place. Elsewhere in the village there are food stalls, jewellery making and, most of all, activities where children and adults put together twigs and tissue paper, paint and glue, to create decorative lanterns. At other stalls banners are made and costumes created from old scraps of material. As I proceed with my kids from stall to stall, from activity to activity, I gain an increasing understanding of the power of the local legend. We feel the power of the layers of story as it is woven into rich, memorable experiences. The day moves towards dusk and more and more people gather. Little groups huddle while other local stories are told as the sun goes down – stories of dragons and magic and mystery, tales vibrant in a swirl of colour and sound and wonder. Then, as the sun sets, the deep boom of a drum begins to thump. Slowly the sound moves closer, relentless against the encroaching night sky. The excited hubbub hushes; the crowded street of people waits and then gently parts as we see the glow of lanterns carried by children and adults from the village, proudly displaying their beacons of light contrasted starkly against the darkening sky. Behind we see a swooping figure, small at first, then larger; with screeching and wailing we catch first sight of the dragon, a black monster with fire-red eyes and long nails, tethered on chains by seven strong men. The paper dragon dips and dives at the crowds, people cheer, people scream, children whoop with delight. The darkness descends, the lanterns form a circle in the grass, capturing the dragon, and the story is completed for another year as the music fades and faces blur back into the night. People return to their homes, full of stories of the day, full of the joys of a day of living, learning, dreaming, touching and tasting.

I have used this story because I believe that it graphically illustrates an important point that lies at the centre of school improvement and also at the heart of this book, namely that the improvement of schools, the approaches, the reasons, the direction that we might take, all depend so much on how we choose to live life and how we see it, either as a series of separate activities or as an integrated holistic experience.

Our schools can be wonderful places of enchantment and creativity, opening doorways to new ways of perceiving, new ways of being; but they are most of all places of exquisite hope in the possibility of the future, in the possibility of people. To me this means we have to choose what is seen to matter and then go out and collectively begin to move towards achieving it. What we choose takes us on one journey, just as what we choose to ignore could take us somewhere else. How we develop our schools so that they capture the richness and vitality of the human spirit is a matter of thinking, living, working and seeing differently, it is a matter of consciousness. If we take a systemic rather than a fragmented view of the world, even if we limit that world to the school world, we recognize that the only really viable solutions to our present challenges are sustainable ones. They have to be ones that satisfy 'needs without diminishing the prospects of future generations' (Brown, 1981). I see this as our great challenge in the coming years in school improvement, to establish sustainable learning communities. Schools will inevitably play a significant part in doing this but they will not do so without a change of mindset. One of the things that struck me on that summer's day in Cornwall was the feeling of being engaged, challenged to be involved and needed in something that was bigger than me. It had a sense of occasion. It got me thinking: why can't learning always be like this, why can't schools be like this? It got me thinking about what type of place I would like to learn in, and whether the schools I had worked in before the holidays reflected any of those characteristics. What do schools value? What matters to them? How are those values challenged by the world outside and reshaped by that world? Is that shaping reflecting what might be best for learners and learning?

Those of you who know me, and know of my work, will know I take quite a different view from those who favour the idea of a 'value-free' (Woodhead, 1998) school improvement and educational reform (which often means little more than condoning the lack of values in the economic orthodoxy of our time). I believe school should liberate the mind and the heart, and that it should emancipate (Fielding, 1996). I remain an eternal optimist despite what many see as insurmountable pressures from outside schools, I maintain a commitment to the local as an advocate of the democratic significance of the local voice within a network that creates its power from deliberated and applied choices based around sustainability. As Jonathan Porritt, the veteran campaigner for ecological issues, recently commented, the power of the local argument is that 'it is explicitly value-driven, and so much the stronger and more inspiring for it' (Porritt, 1996).

My book is based on the assumptions that we face unprecedented change, that if suitable sustainable reform is to be achieved then education will play a major part in the transformation and in that process it too will be transformed, and that education will emerge as a stronger, more value-based expression of lifelong processes of learning, activity and reflection which will better serve all those involved.

I think we can do this, and so my book speaks of hope and ambition and reflects this optimism that we can design and live in a better place than the one we currently occupy. If you know me you will also know that this book has been a long time in the making. Kernels of it have been drafted and redrafted over many years, during which time the ideas have been tried out in school, they have been left to germinate, and they have been revisited and re-evaluated for their impact and effect on how teachers now think, live and see improvement. The insights I have gained from this luxury of time have caused me to think about the unique character of individual schools and how they relate and respond to local circumstances, and how these schools can be considered in a wider reform agenda and treated as a collective group. In examining these ideas I have deliberately used the privileged opportunity of working with senior managers at conferences and workshops throughout the country, as well as maintaining discussions via the phone or by email. During all of that time, because of the relentless pace of educational reform, I have wrestled with matters of purpose and meaning in educational reform and change. This has caused me to reflect critically on what I have done with schools and to ask myself whether some of the arguments I have used to promote inquiring and learning schools continue to address something that matters, something that is sustainable and which carries with it a degree of authenticity.

Inevitably, as in any process, there comes a point when one accepts that this is as far as this particular story will go at the moment, and the page is turned as we move on to the next in the hope of retelling the story in a better way next time. As you read this book you will no doubt begin to form your own view of the applicability and use of the ideas that I am raising. I hope that you reconstruct the book for your own purposes and that in reading it you will be challenged in what you do. I know this will work for some of you, and for others it will not. Accepting this as a fact of reform, I hold to the personal nature of the book. From the outset I felt that I wanted to write a book that captured my view of what was happening in schools I was working with, and how the day-to-day reform process was being interpreted and redesigned to establish a new definition of school for a new era.

My intention is to try and formulate some of the language with which the new voice will speak. To achieve this I will argue why we can't carry on running schools in the way that we do. I will suggest how we might begin to redesign what we currently do with a view to what we might have to confront to make sustainable changes, not necessarily confronting what is focused on at present, but focusing on activity that can give a different interpretation of the purpose of school and can open up a new direction for learning schools to pursue that will suit the dawning of a new age. This agenda is a matter for leaders and followers (Blase and Anderson, 1995). Who they are does not concern me; what they do does. The leaders and followers I am writing about should be both philosophers and mystics (Rabin, 1998): philosophers pursuing truth rationally, mystics pursuing truth intuitively. All else that leaders do is of secondary importance; seeking truth within schools in the form of meaningful, sustainable approaches to living and learning is the primary goal if we are to transform our society from one that will continue to be crippled by the inadequacies of the legacy of the industrial age to one that finds true meaning in the new ecological paradigm. Leaders must do this without apology despite the fact that it might seem and sound a little quirky and out of place; they must do it confidently, quietly, and continually.

I understand that there is a balancing between the search for truth and the practicalities of school life and that this is problematic. It places educators as lead figures in the centre of a swirl of argument and counter-argument on the purpose of school, presenting them with decisions that will have an effect now on students but which may not see their fulfilment for years. It places educators as lead figures at the heart of a moral debate where they have to choose what is right whilst they are faced with the constant demands of external reform – someone else's agenda (Hochschild, 1983). An educator in a lead role has no choice in this matter, she has to commit to one line of development: either to seek answers through instrumental change, or to redesign the problem. As I have indicated, finding immediate answers to complex problems within accountable frameworks is the backdrop to this discussion. I have witnessed that leaders know that sometimes what they do creates the answers required, but that this does not necessarily correspond with what is right. I see the consequences all around, in systems which lack purpose and passion and which control rather than liberate the human spirit. Many of the truly important questions that schools grapple with arise now not as a result of the luxury of reflective time but, if they occur at all, they arise 'on the hoof' amongst a plethora of other, competing demands. This can sap energy and enthusiasm. As a result, truth becomes compromised over other temporal aims of schooling: to service corporate business, to equip the society with the right kind of worker (Carnegie Corporation, 1993). In writing Part 2 of this book I have tried to capture some of the struggle that I believe is being played out in schools as they come to terms with a changing world and as they try to refocus their improvement. To do this I have sought to describe what I see as the crux of the argument within the improvement of schools and to locate this argument within the wider socio-political and socio-cultural climate. As a result I have constructed what might initially feel like two books in one. To create a sense of wholeness and to overcome this disjuncture, I have borrowed the metaphor of a search (Campbell, 1988). I did this because I think it fits with what I am saying about schools making a deliberate choice to embark on an important journey: to do so we prepare, we navigate, we experience, we interpret and observe and we recount and share the experience with others.

The first part of the book seeks to contextualize the main argument. It prepares us for our journey. The second part seeks to illuminate what is happening in practice in response to varied understandings of the implications of the first part; it illustrates steps along the journey. The final part describes some of the challenges that this journey is discovering, and provides some ideas and questions which can serve to guide others in the same direction.

This approach works for me, and has allowed me to explore some of the important themes and issues which the school, like any other important cultural organization, is facing during what I believe is an interface of powerful, differing and competing interpretations of how to proceed in order to grow and develop our organizations and selves within society.

This work reports an evolutionary process still unfolding. That is one reason why I have found the book so hard to write, as I was grappling with a personal journey of understanding how to convey some of these ideas, and how to understand what I was seeing in the work with which I myself was involved. I have begun to realize that as I understand, I am influenced by my understanding. I have come to see that personal growth happens in conjunction with, and not apart from, the specific activity taking place inside individual schools. It remains important to have an idea of destination so as not to become hopelessly lost, but it is not necessary to have that view of the destination completely established. On the contrary, it is necessary to draw upon and use the influences around to inform and enrich the journey. I am reminded of the ancient Chinese tale of journeys, where we take the role of the traveller and fix our mind on where we want to go, we visualize what our destination might look like, and, as we do so, part of us is already there. The time that we then spend carefully moving towards that place is a journey towards wholeness, where we will meet up again with ourselves. In the past this has often been a personal journey; the challenge we face in our schools is to make it a collective one.

This approach is the way I try to work with schools and local education authorities (LEAs). It is responsive to the daily hubbub of activity, but it is also deliberately provocative and challenging, and demands further thinking and attention. It is driven by a desire to search out what matters, to pursue improvement towards lasting and sustainable ways of thinking and undertaking the whole task of teaching and learning. Some headteachers I have met choose to avoid this approach at all costs and opt for what I believe is probably an easier life but what I also believe is a short-term and ultimately unproductive view of improvement, based on isolation and organizational independence. Others stick with it (and stick with me, and for that I thank them!) and commit themselves to acknowledging all the ups and downs of the journey, the frustrating lack of signposts that could help us to make the decisions along the way, and the inevitable frustrations of playing the long game; and as a result they are beginning to demonstrate an organizational characteristic akin to learning. They are in the process, charting new territory (Leithwood, 1992).

The process of starting, thinking, modifying, stopping, redesigning and continuing is not unfamiliar to anyone involved in activity that can be described as school improvement.[1] I'm sure that in your experience of working in schools you will know that they are places often characterized by confusion and mixed messages rather than clarity, by partly developed approaches, by rumour and counter-rumour, with people struggling to keep up with a multiplicity of jobs which never seem to run out and never get completed in the manner in which people really wanted to complete them. On the other hand, teaching in school is full of unexpected and delightful turns, for instance when a student suddenly shows the smile of recognition after struggling, for what seems like weeks but is usually minutes, to make sense of something; or when a parent turns up out of the blue and offers some insight or comment that can add that special touch to the day; or, sometimes, when ideas which have seemingly been divergent and fuzzy (Kosko, 1993) suddenly converge and provide a sense of meaning and purpose which captures people's imagination and drive.

As this book has developed, so too has my renewed sense of purpose and direction in my work with colleagues in schools and with local education authorities in England. It is with them that I have struggled to make sense of the monumental scale of educational reform that is taking place at this time. Through talking about this work I have had the special opportunity to connect with many other colleagues and friends from around the world who are engaged in similar activities, and I have come to recognize where some of the similarities lie, as well as some of the considerable differences (Townsend, Clarke and Ainscow, 1999). These many experiences have allowed me to draw ideas together and to try and make some sense of what school improvement means today inside a climate which calls for continuous improvement and renewal. I have done this because I remain convinced that we will only succeed in making real improvements to our educational system if we change the way in which we think about what we do in and with schools. This requires the courage to think outside the obvious frame of reference and the given ways of examining the present problems that education faces. It demands that something else is offered to those who wish to move in such a direction so that they might begin to talk about another way, and demonstrate that to colleagues who I believe rightly remain sceptical and unconvinced without some examples of ways forward. This book will try to do this. It remains to be seen if you, the reader, will come to the discussion and be moved to participate in that change as a result, whether you will want to add your part to the new map as we sketch out the territory of learning within an emerging learning school system.

WHO IS THIS BOOK FOR?

With these thoughts at the start, who is this book for? Who might profitably take the time out to read it? A book is an incredibly indulgent thing to write. It takes out huge chunks of time, and so, if I'm honest, there is a degree of personal wish-fulfilment involved in the writing. But there is also a genuine desire to connect ideas and to talk about a difficult area to the audience with whom I mainly work, that is, the teachers, headteachers and advisers who are trying to improve the school system on a daily basis.

This book seeks to tread the difficult territory between practitioners and research communities (Miles, 1993). I deliberately want to question and illuminate some of the darker corners of the improvement world in which many of us are working. In particular, I want to raise the profile of some of the issues of concern to so many of the schools and teachers I work with, who want to raise these issues but find that they have few opportunities and channels through which to voice their ideas and questions. These concerns often focus on where improvement work is leading. Of necessity the book therefore grapples with some complex issues. School improvement is a thoroughly complex matter, and I have always shared the view of Seymour Sarason, who stated that 'for any problem there is always a simple solution, which is invariably wrong' (Sarason, 1990). I take this as my starting point, along with some homespun wisdom from my youngest daughter Hannah, who once said to me, 'Dad, why do I have to take "yes" for an answer?'

To inform the book I draw upon a number of projects in which I have had the pleasure to be involved over the past five years. In all of these projects there have been moments of considerable clarity and focus, and there have been moments of confusion and muddle. The agenda for reform is complex, multi-layered and frequently under-conceptualized, and I believe that as a profession educators suffer from this as a result. This book tries in its own way to offer some structure and interpretation of school improvement, focusing particularly on aspects of the work that facilitate a learning school. Whilst this territory is not new (Fullan, 1999), it remains controversial and does not always fit with the present reform agenda within the English system. I believe that this does not in itself matter. A vital point about the meaning of school improvement is that it establishes itself as an emancipatory movement rather than one geared towards the maintenance of the status quo. To do this I believe it is necessary to challenge and engage critically with current operations and seek better ways of doing them, not just to reinforce them or to adhere unquestioningly to the reformers' demands. This places the role of the school improver which I advocate in the centre of the debate about the 'future' of schools, in a political, critical and participatory role. As Aristotle was reported to have said: 'It is the role of the citizen to keep his mouth open!' I maintain that it is the role of the school improver to do the same and to question, challenge and generally be the truth seeker, at a time when many are happy to settle for second best because it is easier that way. If you are interested in the mechanics of maintaining what you already do, don't read this book; you won't find anything helpful in it. If however, you are interested in how to use challenge, critique and conversation to create learning schools within learning communities, then read on; it might help you do that. The experiences documented in this book identify some practical approaches to improvement that can be taken with the purpose of changing the dynamics of the school environment without damaging the sensitive network of relationships and friendships that schools always need in order to function.

THE STRUCTURE OF THIS BOOK

Finally, I have already mentioned something about the structure of the book, which is shaped around a journey of three parts. The first part of the journey is about preparedness and is focused on the design of learning schools, the second part of the journey is based on the development of the learning school, and the third part concerns the challenges that face us as we move into this new territory of the learning system. As the book proceeds, the key concepts for each chapter are recalled at the end of the chapter. It is my sincere hope that as these concepts connect, what emerges is an argument for learning schools within a learning system. Its themes are: knowledge about change, a vision of a learning school and what that might mean, culture, the school as a community, and sustainability. As I visit each of these themes I will provide some examples of work in progress that is having an effect in positive ways on the thinking and practice of improvement for sustainability and learning.

In the spirit of inquiry and collegiality I have used the first person throughout this book. I know it is not orthodox (for a fascinating analysis of language and power see Fairclough, 1989), but it suits me, as I can hear myself and my voice better when writing that way. When I use 'we' I mean me and you, if you are willing to come along on the journey, otherwise replace 'we' with 'they'; you will not have as much fun, but you might still get through the book!

I maintain from the outset that I believe schools are communities and not service industries (Sergiovanni, 1992). They therefore have value bases different to those of competitive business and corporate multi-site organizations, because they have a local user base (Starratt, 1995). This is a simple statement but one that I believe has profound significance in the context of current educational reform. In developing the idea of schools as communities and not service industries or production lines we begin to see that their 'stuff' is people, adults and young people, and their territory is 'learning', and 'learning for living', daily, communally – and it will be argued in this book – with a real sense of purpose about creating a better future.

NOTE

1   I will use Hopkins, Ainscow and West's definition of improvement here, to mean 'an approach to educational change that has the twin purposes of enhancing student achievement and strengthening the school's capacity for managing change' (Hopkins *et al.*, 1994, p. 68).

Part 1: Thinking About the Journey Ahead

Chapter 1

Searching for Improvement

There is something immensely affirming about a Gothic cathedral, rising as it does above its city and landscape, dwarfing its surroundings by comparison. It is a constant reminder of a transcendent reality against which all else pales and through which all has access and meaning. For centuries the Gothic cathedral stood as a profound outer expression of a living faith that the world made ultimate sense and possessed a wholeness accessible to everyone as part of creation. The Gothic cathedral spoke a language of image and metaphor, and stood as living symbol of a unified sense of reality for its age.

Yet the cathedral was a vertical image, an inspiring testimony to a vertically conceived God, to a spirituality of transcendence in which the soul sought refuge above and beyond the realities of this world. The soul's eye and reach were directed upwards past the flying butresses and arches and vaulted ceilings, past the towers and spires, to meet the embrace of a God beyond the tangible. If there was unity, it was a unity imposed from above by virtue of precedence, hierarchy, levels of reality, and transcendence. It was to be found at the end of a search, a pilgrimage, a holy journey.

What still remains for us of the Gothic vision of wholeness is the legacy of a search, now transposed to a world whose transcendent markers have been dwarfed by new vertical strivings for power, achievement, knowledge, and accomplishment. Our skyscrapers and rockets take our reaching to the heavens, not to meet there the hope of a gift of meaning but to celebrate striving itself. How is the search for a sense of wholeness to be achieved in a world whose speciality is specialisation, whose language is linear and literal, and whose sense of the symbolic is derived from cartoon and caricature? How is the search for wholeness to be expressed in a world made horizontal by the sheer immensity of our knowledge about this world?

Linda Olds, *Metaphors of Interrelatedness*

DEFINING THE SEARCH: CONCEPTIONS AND MISCONCEPTIONS OF OUR AGE

This book has been written at a time when humanity faces serious global challenge to change its ways of operating. To provide a context and a backdrop to this discussion and by way of indicating my position as the writer, I will make the following assumptions.

Society is in the midst of crisis and heading for an 'ecological abyss' (Earth Summit, Rio, 1992). It is driven by an unsustainable form of economic growth and there is urgent need to stop and re-orientate. This reorientation will happen anyway, but it needs to happen sooner rather than later, and it therefore requires political choices to be made by people inside local communities, with the appropriate forms of external support, to transform society into a sustainable form. Reorientation requires new ways of thinking about the problems we face. The solution has to be sustainable, and it has to be integrative rather than individualistic if we are to avoid walking exactly the road that is leading us to the ecological abyss in the first place. Systemic strategic thinking (Townsend, 1995), with the education system playing a key role in the process of transformation, is a key to this process. In playing the role, education will itself be transformed.

Educators are currently in the midst of a plethora of changes, and as these changes unfold inside schools they create tensions as well as new opportunities, which schools have to deal with and overcome. I argue in this book that the tensions arise from a dynamic interplay between paradigms – each representing competing ways of seeing and valuing the reality of the school and its place in society. This conflict is between the modern paradigm, characterized by individualistic and mechanistic practice, and an ecological paradigm in the process of emerging, which values integrated wholeness. Those who seek understanding of change by looking at the constituent parts favour the modern approach to reform. This has been portrayed as a 'value-free' system but in reality it has been colonized by free-market values (Troman, 1989) which renounce progressive educational values in favour of 'induction into a harsh, unforgiving, competitiveness-at-all-costs economy' (Porritt, 1996). Those who look to the change across the whole system seek integrated wholeness; it is an intrinsically value-driven approach to systemic change and, in my opinion, much the better for it.

The emphasis on parts has been the modern focus of educational reform. It has dominated the ways of thinking about educational change for the major part of this century and it is now rapidly becoming the discredited view being forced onto our time.

Emerging from the new sciences (Bateson, 1979; Goodwin, 1994) from the early part of the twentieth century onwards came the emphasis on understanding the whole called ecological, holistic or systemic thinking (Capra, 1996) (I will use these terms synonymously). This way of thinking has focused attention on systems being integrated and searches for patterns to facilitate understanding of how systems interrelate and make sense.

As we begin to turn the corner into a new century, there is an ongoing desire to understand and to apply the most appropriate approaches to the operation of our human systems. We do this in order to meet the challenges of the times, and to do so with a method that is consistent with these challenges. To be most suitable, this method needs to be adaptive and evolving rather than predefined and linear.

Paradoxically, the mechanistic modern paradigm is projecting human inquiry towards the ecological because the rational analysis of the present system necessitates synthesis and holistic comprehension in preference to the limitations of reductionist linear viewpoints. It is, I believe, an inevitable historical and evolutionary process to move understanding of social systems towards the ecological viewpoint. Here lies a core question of my book, What is the purpose of school improvement inside this arena – to maintain, or to transform? I side with the latter.

QUESTIONS

I started the chapter with the long quote from Linda Olds' book, *Metaphors of Interrelatedness* (1992), because I believe that she raises two central questions concerning the searches we are embarking upon as we make a transition from the modern to the ecological paradigm. These questions indicate where some of the tensions and differences between the two paradigms lie:

- How is the 'search' for wholeness to be expressed within our schools so that staff and students might make a personal and a collective sense of what it is that they are moving into and participating in, rather than being bystanders in someone else's plan, made insignificant and voiceless by the sheer immensity of the system?
- How is the 'search' for a sense of wholeness to be achieved in a school system which has built itself on the maintenance of artificial boundaries and subject specialisms, where the environments in which we establish and focus what we call learning are controlled by linear structures and where the specialisms serve to fragment, disassemble and inhibit the construction of integrated meaning?

Two features emerge, the 'expression' and the 'achievement' of a changed view of human systems – in our case, the school. What might the expression of a learning school, operating in transition towards an ecological paradigm, look like? And, how might we begin to make the changes necessary to get us there?

The changes required are to move from the individualized view of schooling, where learners experience their education as a product driven along by efficiently managed schools that see results in the form of outcome performance, through to a new type of school, one that can learn from its actions and develop ways of working that re-norm the school to develop more ecologically compatible systemic practice.

We know that there are other ways of proceeding that can equip us to live with uncertainty, that can help us to cope with the fact that there will be questions for which our expertise provides no answers. We know that there are other ways of undertaking the learning journey which account for emerging, uncertain, more holistic comprehension (Claxton, 1997). These ways require a different way of thinking about learning. As Rilke wrote:

> Everything is gestation and bringing forth. To let each impression
> and each germ of a feeling come to completion wholly in itself, in the
> dark, in the inexpressible, the unconscious, beyond the reach of
> one's own intelligence, and await with deep humility and patience
> the birth-hour of a new clarity: that alone is living the artist's life.
> Being an artist means not reckoning and counting, but ripening like
> the tree which does not force its sap, and stands confident in the
> storms of spring without the fear that after them may come no
> summer. It does come. But it comes only to the patient, who are
> there as though eternity lay before them, so unconcernedly still and
> wide. (Rilke, 1986)

The sentiments expressed here are a feature of many educators' and parents' belief that the learning process is something that cannot be forced. It is, rather, a way of thinking, seeing, living and working as a lifelong process. Yet this view of learning is not the one that has been advanced inside the present paradigm. Learning at the present time is still geared almost exclusively towards the workplace, it is shallow and decontextualized, and it serves the economic production objectives of society.

WAYS OF SEEING THE JOURNEY

In his recent book, the philosopher Jean Baudrillard (1994) describes what he calls the 'dance of the fossils'. He uses this metaphor to illustrate the predominant way in which modern societies think and interpret the world, which in due course also influences the manner in which such societies proceed to act. What characterizes Baudrillard's description is his portrayal of the way that these institutions undertake their plans, policies and practices. He suggests that established institutions, among which we can include schools, characterize the dominant thinking of their times. This focus is on the maintenance of present systems, rather than the development of new ones, and because of this they seek to manage rather than to develop our conceptual grasp of a changing environment. Citing such examples as the demand for management and measurement of performance, Baudrillard argues that efforts to establish order and control over all manner of human activity in the workplace are a legacy of a modern view of power operating through hierarchical structures. The result is an illusion of certainty that manipulates popular opinion to believe that it is possible to seek out simple, technical solutions to solve the complex, systemic problems that society faces.

Baudrillard writes that the millennium represents an illusion of the end of a particular period of time, but highlights the fact that this change in time has a symbolic meaning representing a transition from one epoch of thinking to another. The possible change in thinking about how people might function in a global society, as a result of profound changes in the organization and habits of both social and economic life, corresponds – not coincidentally, he suggests – with the emergence of the new millennium.[1]

The advent of this new millennium has brought with it thinking about how we should reconstruct our view of the purpose and even the need for schools. Much of the present-day improvement activity within schools and school systems concerns itself with the improvement of technical issues related to the task of enhancing organizational and pupil performance. However, in a transformational improvement agenda, it becomes important that attention is given to both the meaning and purpose of schooling and its relationship to learning. Whilst this maintains attention on what the organization and the learners actually do, it raises new issues and challenges for us to consider.

As ideas evolve about how to see the world in more integrated ways and the modern paradigm is being challenged (Huckle and Sterling, 1996), we are able to identify the emergence of different ways of thinking about reality, and the different values that might underpin that thinking. What we notice from Table 1.1

Table 1.1: *Individualistic and integrative – values and thinking in transition*

Values		Thinking	
Individualistic	**Integrative**	**Individualistic**	**Integrative**
expansion	conservation	rational	intuitive and rational
competition	co-operation	analysis	synthesis and analysis
quantity	quality	reductionist	holistic
domination	partnership	linear	non-linear

Source: Adapted from Capra, F. (1996) *The Web of Life*. London: HarperCollins.

is that individualistic values are generally related to the use of power through domination over other people (Blase and Anderson, 1995) in the form of hierarchical organizational structures. A social structure such as a school, built around a hierarchy, will reflect these individualistic values and will fear and resist a system that advances a different kind of power structure.

If we start to consider what schools might need to do to continue to improve on their present trajectory (Gray *et al.*, 1999), we see that they will eventually come to a point where they need to communicate and examine what other schools are doing. They are naturally drawn to do this as they operate as communities (Townsend, 1994). In order for this to be successful it is far easier for the school to establish working partnerships with other local schools, to work on co-operative activity and to share findings (Clarke, 1999a and b; Hargreaves, 1999) than it is to pursue individualistic agendas and attempt to gain from what others are doing. The value base that drives schools towards sharing practice and establishing learning teams is integrative, it is a representative symbol of the emerging ecological paradigm in action. The most suitable power arrangement to facilitate mutual learning is power practised through influence, and the most suitable structure to facilitate this kind of system is a network, not a hierarchy.

THE CHALLENGE – TO MAKE CHOICES AND TO COMMIT TO ACTION

I want to suggest that there are profound challenges facing educational reform which are currently held in abeyance and are not enabled to be fully examined, debated and engaged with because the power of the established system is exercised over the one that is emerging (Saul, 1997). These challenges, when pursued, begin to redefine the meaning and purpose of schools, pointing them towards ever greater democratic activity geared to supporting learning at the personal, organizational and wider community levels. This is in direct antithesis to the corporate, economic objective, where the passivity and conformity of the individual is paramount for an efficient workforce. Every important characteristic of Western individualism preceded the main economic events of the last three centuries (Saul, 1998). It was the human-centred characteristics that created social systems and made democratic society what it is. We need to revitalize the voices of participants in change whilst challenging them to redesign their system on values and purposes suited to the real needs of our time. These challenges are broader than the technical solution (Codding, 1997; Commons, 1985) which school effectiveness has left as its legacy, and reflect widespread features of contemporary life, the stuff of which many people are struggling to make sense.

FINDING A PURPOSE FOR IMPROVEMENT

In my own work I have become involved in exploring how to revitalize and inspire schools as places of learning with a sense of purpose and ambition. This work explores and makes transparent (Oatley, 1992) the ideas, doubts, concerns and questions that teachers raise as they pursue their daily working lives. As we do this together, we examine what these ideas say about the way that the school is enabling or inhibiting learning. We explore how the choices that are being made in the form of strategic plans are representing either maintenance or transformative ways of working. We might do this by reflecting on teaching material, or on the teaching approaches which they know are not engaging learners and lighting 'fires' in the imagination,[2] but turning learners off and away from school. In pursuing these concerns and questions I have found that something else happens, however: teachers and learners rekindle their own spirit to learn and to feel that they have a place to play in the design of their school, rather than being the onlookers. In this work I have come to believe that we face both organizational and personal challenges and choices that concern the purpose and process of schooling. This is led by a changing demand for school function, to explore what we might mean by sustainable communities where social, cultural and physical environments are established which support and satisfy the need for the human curiosity and challenge but at the same time notice and respond to the ecological implications of economic growth and the future generations (Clarke, Reed and Lodge, 1998).

As I have worked with schools and have raised these issues with teachers and students I have come to believe that this renewed sense of organizational purpose implies change in the process by which we might improve schools and needs a new improvement language with which to focus our search.

If we begin to think of the school as a place of relationships, connections and contexts understood through practice, principles and spirit, our understanding of school changes from the mechanistic towards an appreciation of the whole learner and the whole learning environment of the school as the necessary focus of improvement effort. Some of the experiences that are then raised by the investigation of important features of social living are constructed by schools for students so that they can undertake a safe simulation (Hargreaves, 1994) and can usefully deconstruct them and talk about them and make more sense of what they experience outside school in daily life. But we appreciate, too, that many of the ways in which the school might 'teach' students about the world they are growing up in are serendipitous, they happen by chance, and therefore teachers need to be aware of the possibility that these learning opportunities can be used, nurtured and revealed in order to develop a new understanding of what it is to learn and to grow in human society. Some of this agenda necessarily addresses power, choice, voice and the role of the citizen in beyond-modern society.

I believe that this view of formal education sees learning as having a transformational and developmental potential. From the practical matters of educating people to be literate and numerate so that they can function and participate in a democratic society, to the applied uses of critical engagement in then changing communities through collective action, education has a central emancipatory role (Illich and Verne, 1976).

To view education as both an emancipatory and a transformational experience for students demands a perspective on what we might do with schools and how we might go about what we do. It is a significant leap from the school reform of the present and it raises implications for what the school of the future might look like and how it might function. It suggests a need for a new pedagogy that has as its core an understanding of life in social settings in the form of competences and an identification of important life themes, rather than having school activity designed around the transmission of subject knowledge. The school should enable learners to link together the lessons we have learnt at our cost in the past century, so that there is a sense of connection between learner and the natural environment, learner and social responsibility, learner and work, learner and learning, learner and the sense of self. The improvement of education for learning lies in two features of present educational improvement activity: the first is concerned with values and purpose, the second concerns action. However, instead of wasting time and effort tinkering with the modern constructions of school, I believe that meaningful improvement activity requires us to rethink how we might proceed to create a new system and not to accept that the present directions are correct or appropriate for the demands we collectively face to shift paradigms from modern to ecological.

I also believe that the changes represent longer-term realities as schools move their organizational activity towards learning and away from schooling. Senge (Senge, 1990; Senge *et al.*, 1994) argues that our school system suffers from 'learning disabilities'. These disabilities inhibit the ability to see the problems we face with an open mind. Instead we are plagued by the habits, inferences and ineffective past experiences which serve to inform our interpretations of the present and to drive us to 'maintain and tinker' (Fullan, 1991) rather than to transform.

As in many other established professions, there are patterns of working and long-established beliefs and values which underpin both personal and organizational life. These are rarely articulated; they are, however, widespread and taken for granted (Argyris, 1990). Teachers frequently draw on these beliefs and values as a basis and justification for the way they go about their work, as they represent an underlying purpose and rationale, but they remain personal and individualized inside the modern paradigm, having little power or influence. The mixed messages teachers receive from external requirements from government, calling for reform in what they do whilst maintaining and exceeding present levels of pupil performance, causes them considerable anxiety as change challenges their values and beliefs, taking them further away from the teacher/learner relationship based around care, concern and shared investigation to a service role, devoid of the human touch.

> *I used to have time for the kids I worked with. I could sit with them and listen to their stories and their observations on what was happening inside and outside school. The relationships I now have with my class are so different, I know one or two of them really well, but an in-depth relationship, knowing how they are trying to make sense of things, is something I just never seem to manage to get time for anymore ... the responsibility has shifted from working with children as learners to filling in forms and administrating curriculum changes. The job seems to have has lost its heart in the attempt to improve standards and I'm not sure if that is such a good thing in the long run.*
>
> *(Teacher of Year 5, June 1999)*

Often, the management cry is that staff will not change, but instead exhibit what is interpreted as resistance (Clarke, 1996; Hochschild, 1983). Often the teachers' response is simply to argue a different point of view that simply cannot be heard, or cannot be afforded to be heard inside the present paradigm. As Toffler (1970) commented more than a quarter of a century ago, there is a 'crisis of organization' in the public and private sectors which goes on, unperceived yet systemically active: 'most organizations have a structure that was designed to solve problems that no longer exist' (p. 124).

Teachers expressing different viewpoints open up, rather than close down, the capacity for change because they raise the possibility of an alternative view. Creating situations where the voices of those who have little power – teachers, students and parents - can be heard broadens improvement potential. Toffler (1970) maintains that 'anticipating probable futures' is only part of what needs doing if we are to shift the emphasis and infuse the entire society with a greater sense of tomorrow. He suggests that we need to vastly widen our conception of possible futures, developing a multiplicity of possibilities, of potential tomorrows, and that conjecture, speculation and vision are as coldly and practically necessary as 'feet-on-the-floor realism' was in earlier times.

CRISIS – OR DENIAL OF CRISIS?

I would like to suggest that perhaps, in what I want to call the modern configuration, this might be as good as it gets in those schools that are already operating at high levels of performance. Those demonstrating less coherent and structured approaches have some catching up to do within this modern paradigm, but the logic of the present reform agendas suggests that once undertaking improvement activity in ways that have now well and truly been investigated, they too will catch up and optimize their capacity under the present constraints.

So what we witness might be interpreted as a crisis, or for some a denial of crisis because it suits to maintain what already exists rather than develop. The crisis is in the form of an optimized system, classically (Kuhn, 1970) a point of paradigm shift as more and more people will seek an alternative solution through which they can continue to grow. The solution for an optimized system does not lie in continuing to play around with a few variables such as management approaches, or even in redesigning parts of the curriculum whilst assuming that the underlying structure is sound. What is required is a fundamental shift of that underlying structure upon which 'schooling' is based. It has to move into an understanding of integrated learning and away from the individualized, simplistic, piece-by-piece approach to reform. Within this observation is a significant feature of the crisis: a lack of conjecture, speculation and vision from the grassroots and an overwhelming amount of it from external agencies.

The story that unfolds as we attempt to make sense of what is happening and why is one that identifies the dynamic tensions in play between reform and practice. It raises the need to explore territory towards which schools might move in the future, concerned with our two questions (Olds, 1992): the search for an expression of wholeness, and the achievement of wholeness.

In order to maintain a sense of balance as we learn about new ways of thinking, seeing, living and working in our schools we have to also unlearn. We have to lose the baggage of the past. To do this we have to make collective choices about what to lose and share a sense of what we might want to achieve. This is, as Louis (1994) says, a political choice. Schools must first decide to act, and then decide how they might want to act.

> Educational systems are expected to be everything for everybody,
> irrespective of other national or cultural differences, and schools
> often become the scapegoat for almost every social, cultural,
> economic and political solution. Selecting a new vision of schooling

11

tisfy all constituencies and meet all of the expressed goals
ble. What this means is that any school restructuring has to
particularly difficult challenge of political selection before it
o settle into a new routine of learning.
is, 1994, p.15)

MANAGEMENT TO LEADERSHIP

To develop schools to the point of making conscious choices is to ask them to display considerable leadership skill. As Schlechty (1990) comments, 'the process of taking on bigger, more complex changes to achieve significant improvement means that failure is more likely on occasions'. Under the constraints of the present system the experience of failure is considered catastrophic and to be avoided at all costs. Yet failure is a part of learning just as success is. Inside an integrative organizational environment, the conscious recognition and use of the experience of failure as a result of deliberate action and inquiry can lead to new designs and new conceptualization of persistent problems. Inevitably, it implies learning about how the school 'learns', and how it responds organizationally to different challenges.

Schlechty (1990) points to the important role that leaders must take in designing and supporting a learning system that purposefully adopts an attitude towards the acceptance and use of risk: 'leaders must learn how to maximise the potential for success just as so many have learnt how to minimise the opportunity to fail'. Systemic thinking assists educators in maximizing their capacity (Stoll *et al.*, 1999) to learn and the practice of such thinking in turn relies upon leadership and leaders to grasp some of the salient messages of systems thinking and to have the skills and facility to realize its implications.

Inside learning schools, there is a collective recognition that leadership is a responsibility of the whole system and not merely of those who are currently seen as being in charge under the modern hierarchical structures. There has to be activity that recognizes that everyone has a role to play in making changes happen that enhance personal and collective activity. However, at this stage in the transition towards an ecological paradigm, I think we are on the interface between the individualistic and the integrative, and as a result we experience working tensions over how the individual inside the school 'sees', 'works' and 'thinks' about improvement (Badaracco and Ellsworth, 1989). What many schools experience as a result at the moment is the whirling effect of combinations of approaches they can go with and those they cannot, which is repeated as a pattern at the school level and which in turn influences the individual understanding and vision. (See Figure 1.1.)

It is of importance that these tensions, these differences in viewpoint between individual and school and within the community of the school begin to be looked at, for they illuminate what is being contested and give insights into what people value and believe in, as an understanding of their meaning, and a willingness to establish the climate for different voices to be heard, will play a central role in creating the necessary conditions for any transition of the school from one system to another. This means more than merely creating staff who have classroom exceeding roles (MacGilchrist *et al.*, 1995), although that is a start, it concerns a frame of mind, an 'organizational consciousness' if you like, that is shared amongst all people in the school.

Schools engaged in initiatives that are replacing modern organizational views of management dominated through linearity and hierarchy are turning to leadership styles that provide more appropriate influential models upon which to develop connections between common interests across different organizational configurations (Binney and Williams, 1995). These reflect changes in the use of power to promote ways of looking at the school so that it serves both the individual and the community but at the expense of neither. (See box on p. 14.)

As the opening statement of this chapter suggests (Olds, 1992), we are in a period of redefining. Just as the medieval world once turned to the use of stone to express its understanding of reality, we must look towards the building blocks of our time in order to capture the essence of what we are about as human beings. Our conceptual building blocks are not the same as those of the past, and while our themes might remain consistent, our interpretation of them evolves and initiates new challenges.

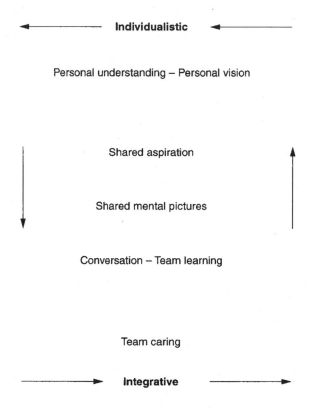

Figure 1.1: *Personal and collective tensions inside learning schools*
Source: Boyle and Clarke, 1998

> *In a small primary school in a deprived part of Bury, the staff had for some time expressed concern at the low levels of literacy amongst the children in the early years of school, and after attempting many literacy courses and applying ideas they still felt that they were not getting to the core of the problem. The headteacher and the literacy co-ordinator initiated a series of parent coffee mornings, where the parents could call in to the school informally and talk to the teachers about literacy and the role school played, and how the teachers would like parents to become involved. The idea was to develop a paired reading initiative, but something quite different emerged. The parents told the teachers that they felt hopelessly inadequate to support their children, as they were barely literate themselves. In response the school initiated a series of support programmes in school time with the aid of the local community group and adult learning service. The initiative was an instant success: large numbers of parents attended and wanted more. The school pursued this and with help from other agencies established an accredited course for parents to attend and gain qualifications. Within a year a number of parents had learnt to read and write, and, significantly, the teachers identified dramatic improvement in the literacy activity of the children. The initiative gained a firmer footing and became one of a number of LEA-funded projects for the coming year to enhance school/community links in positive learning-orientated ways.*

Beare, Slaughter and Jones (1995) identify a series of such key learning themes which are open to changing interpretations:

- Political: globalization and democracy, the role of the individual as a citizen;
- Economic: changes in the industrial base of society, the information age;
- Ecological: the need for sustainability, the recognition of ecological crisis;
- Social: changes in family and community structures;
- Spiritual: what it is to be human; the role of belief and values;
- Technological: the information revolution in the service of human growth;
- Scientific: cognition – how the brain learns; complexity – models to inform human systems analysis.

What is it that makes our interpretations of these themes change? Capra (1996, p. 37) suggests:

> In the shift from mechanistic thinking to systems thinking, the relationship between the parts and the whole has been reversed. Cartesian science believed that in any complex system, the behaviour of the whole could be analysed in terms of the properties of its parts. Systems science shows that living systems cannot be understood by analysis. The properties of the parts are not intrinsic properties, but can be understood only within the context of a larger whole. Thus systems thinking is 'contextual' thinking; and since explaining things in terms of their context means explaining them in terms of their environment, we can also say that all systems thinking is environmental thinking.

School improvement has missed this fundamentally important point by putting an overwhelming emphasis on internal conditions. This suited political agencies, as they could individualize each school and charge it with absolute accountability to its students (Apple, 1998). In an integrative system we have to account for environment while also accounting for actions within the school. It exceeds present demands but reorientates them towards a mutually necessary and beneficial networking based on the identification of localized successes.

The multiplicity of possible ways of gathering, linking and using information with a network 'mindset' liberates improvement activity. It enables new ways of seeing the school world and moves us away from surface levels of analysis towards deeper levels of contextualized understanding.

RETHINKING OUR ROUTE MAP: REDESIGNING CHANGE FROM A CENTRALIZED TO A LOCALIZED POWER BASE

Where situations of change are complex and strategic thinking cannot be concentrated in one location, we see that the 'implementors become formulators' (Mintzberg, 1994), where strategy is found to be most effectively made 'by people who implement it'. It is in these complex situations that the people on the ground should champion the direction of the organization.

The last two decades have brought considerable changes in the way in which schools are managed and structured between the school and the state, but there is little real evidence of any fundamental change in thinking as regards any real shift in the power relations between learner and teacher, school and state. Almost every school system in the world has undergone substantial alterations to its governance, with the dominant trend being decentralization to the school level of some processes previously undertaken centrally (Townsend, Clarke and Ainscow, 1999).

Whilst these reforms have initiated a local accountability they have quite simply failed to enable the local 'implementors' become true 'formulators'. Instead, we have a situation where there is a considerable gap between those who formulate and those who implement, with gestures of local accountability unconnected to any real power to decide. As a result we have a way to go before current reform fundamentally challenges the power base that plagues progress related to learning at a personal or institutional level. This matters because the taking of power by local communities, where local people have a direct say in the activity of the school, is an important democratic and liberating process (Freire, 1974; Apple, 1983) and would enhance the role of the student in the negotiation of learning. It is part of the ecological paradigm's emerging configuration.

In taking managerial rather than pedagogical reform as the principal driver for change, school improvement activity has, with a few exceptions, reinforced the need for a safe, predictable system maintained by strong centralized curriculum and accountability frameworks. I believe that this has happened in part because the focus of school effectiveness and improvement has been naively ignorant of the micro-political complexity of what happens between schools and their communities. As a result, methods have been adopted which assume a view of school reality which is unproblematic and uncontested. This conceptual view of schools has led to improvement being superficial, and instrumental and consisting of an ultimately fruitless series of changes with little or no resonance for those who are daily involved in the process of understanding and dealing with the complex reality of learning at the local level.

So what we witness in a good deal of current reform efforts are increasingly desperate, scattergun attempts to force an old design to make a difference at a national level within a tired system.

Where I see schools that are beginning to take new steps into an as yet undetermined learning-centred future, I am finding that their activity champions grass-roots strategic formulation of change; it is different from what schools are centrally being told is the way forward. The grass-roots formulation is based on localized choice and emphasizes the importance of:

- **Listening to local agendas**: This implies undermanagement rather than overmanagement. In periods of change it is important to allow strategic conversations and activity to emerge and initiate rather than to force an organizational pattern too soon.
- **Designing in systems to tackle difference**: This assumes that anyone can initiate strategic action and schools cannot plan *when* strategies will emerge, they just will. What schools have to develop is the capacity to problematize difference and use it constructively within their local setting so that they can learn to hear one another in the locality, raising issues about working with learners, and to be open to identifying what is happening and when it is working, even if it runs counter-intuitively to the norm of the organization,
- **Seeking patterns**: Schools have supportive approaches to enabling staff to describe practice and connect it with colleagues' approaches in order to establish common emergent patterns.
- **Developing the ability to act and to choose**: This emphasizes both conscious and accidental, or managed and unmanaged, processes that schools adopt in order to enable the ideas to flow through the school that can inform people of the most suitable ways to move forward in their work. These might be deliberate, or they might not, but once they begin to matter, they become more formally structured into the school's life.
- **A freeflowing and emergent approach to strategy**: This tends to occur in times of change. Schools that acknowledge change and recognize it happening will know that in periods of intense development they will undergo a great deal of risk-taking and turbulent activity which will ebb and flow over a school year. Using this knowledge helps them to cope better with their local micro-political activity.
- **Recognizing the 'constitutional configuration'**: This is a question of knowing when to intervene and when not; it is about using established ways of working, and it is about formulating quite new approaches and through these approaches establishing a 'constitutional configuration' of the school. Fundamentally, this is necessary to continue to let ideas flow in a learning school.

Intervention is the art of knowing which journeys are worth taking, and which lead to nowhere.

FINDING YOUR FEET

This grass-roots agenda represents a delicate balancing act. It implies an aware-ness amongst staff of the competing influences and contested nature of educational reform. Particularly it raises the problems that exist between approa-ches to learning that come from outside the school and how these are translated into activity inside the school, so that teachers can think, challenge and respond to the external agent of change.

It is, as we will see later in this book, a profoundly difficult balance to get right (Clarke, 1999a). Too much external pressure in the form of individualistic man-dated reform results in suspicion and in schools left feeling disengaged and disempowered to take control of their own destiny. Too little integrative support through the creation of intra-school systems such as networks can lead to schools becoming complacent and accepting their present performance as an accepted organizational norm.

Mkhatshwa (1999) argues that the balance between what governments and school systems are expected to do and what schools themselves are expected to do is starting to shift. It is shifting from an interventionist stance towards an accountability stance, but to make the move make sense, the power associated with who owns learning, at the organizational and the student levels has to be relocated. Rethinking that balance so as to ensure that appropriate supportive contributions are made at both the macro- and micro-political levels, whilst politicizing the debate to focus attention on the importance of education as a subversive and emancipatory activity, is a matter of crucial significance and relevance to all people as participant citizens in a democratic society. As Thomas Jefferson once said, 'We must trust the expediency of the people'.

What we observe at present seems to me to be very different, a situation of little explicit trust in the people charged with carrying out change. Because of this lack of trust, educational change is presented as neutral material, which is treated as unproblematic and deconstructed into bite-sized pieces for easy consumption because the state dare not let it become a real debate. The core material, be it curriculum reform or leadership 'training', is consequently overly technicized, decontaminated of controversy and critique and reduced to a series of technical activities which professionals then have to administer (Dreyfus and Rabinow, 1983). The result, as Fielding (1996) reminds us, is a loss of the 'richly textured fabric of once familiar educational discourse . . . drained of much of its life, colour and substance'.

This leads to an education system spiralling into crisis through denial of crisis, where the solution to the crisis seems to be to do 'more, louder and harder' (Garmston and Wellman, 1995). Mechanisms are established to avoid discussion on things that matter. These might be concerned with principles, power groups, or the purpose of schools. Instead, we experience a day-to-day denial of persistent underlying problems and concerns about learning. Avoidance and deliberate

17

obstruction of debate on the deeper significance of the learning system so profoundly influence organizational life that they cannot be ignored any longer if progress towards the learning school is going to be made. The only thing worse than having these defences to the debate is living with the denial of their existence. What this all boils down to is a need for change, both in approach and in understanding. The persistence of organizational defences and their denial blinds us to improvements and also to the fact that we are successfully designing our own blindness.

PARADOXES OF CHANGE

It seems vital to me that we should not let the conservatism within the system inhibit the experiments that will promote newer ways of proceeding. The problems that alternatives raise, however, are full of paradox, because the people who lead through and out of crisis are themselves trapped inside the current hegemony. The track record of reform in schools has seen a significant rise in managerial competences, with more effective systems at a whole school level, but often with little or no subsequent teacher effect. As Cuban (1995) reminds us, those same people who have gained success in the present system face the considerable challenge of redesigning and changing track so as to ensure that teachers gain more territorial space to pursue learning rather than schooling agendas, as these will inevitably encroach on managerial space, which is the domain of the current school leaders. If our present system has served to empower management systems, which in turn have maintenance procedures at their core, they will invariably resist the growth of learning systems which have development at theirs (Senge, 1990). I would suggest that the 'classroom exceeding' activity of the mid-1980s and onwards, driven by co-ordination roles and middle management structures, now serves to inhibit the learning system because it has cast teachers in the dual role of manager and instructor. Consequently, and paradoxically, teachers are often less rather than more inclined to innovate and initiate in their work with learners. They are less willing to lead because they live inside the individualistic shell of managerial pre-planned and 'risk-free' cultures, where the next inspection and the anticipation of the next reform wipe out many opportunities for constructive collective activity focused on change to pedagogic practice. I suggest that this present view of educational change has done little to inform and create a professional base of knowledge about pedagogy in varied organizational settings. Instead, we witness teachers as isolated technicians and headteachers often stuck in the role of managers, attempting to introduce someone else's incoherent vision of a future school. We have come to the end of a journey – we have reached the end of the corridor!

So it is as a matter of necessity that I turn to a rethinking of the school, and an examination, with the community of the school, of the form and expression of that rethinking, so as to establish something on which they can come together, something they can believe in and which will benefit them. This has to be a coherent and achievable agenda, but it should also, as Yeats says, 'light the fires of the imagination'.

To begin the journey and the search in this book, I raise some questions that I often ask students, teachers, senior managers and advisers, getting varying degrees of response ranging from the enthusiastic to the negative. How might we conceptualize the future school? How might thinking about it influence the work taking place today in schools so that we can begin to build a future in which we might wish to live and work? These questions form the basis of the next chapter.

KEY ISSUES AND IDEAS IN THIS CHAPTER

- We are living through a period of considerable redefinition of the role, function and purpose of many of our previously cherished institutions as a result of profound changes in access to knowledge and information across the planet.
- As one of these important institutions, the school is itself under redefinition and redesign. It is argued that under the present arrangements the system is fully operationalized, and hence the system is moving into crisis as it has nowhere to go under the current conceptualization.
- The process of redesign in response to this crisis is, however, a contested one. Drawing from what we know about reforms and change (Fullan, 1991) we can usefully apply the 'ready–fire–aim' principle and begin to ask ourselves: What now is the purpose of the school?
- In considering the purpose of schools we can ask whether our improvements are concerned with the maintenance of the present system or the creation of a new one. Examples of this interface of two conflicting systems can be seen in schools that fear change, feel inhibited in their risk-taking and are unwilling to co-operate for fear of other schools improving on the shared knowledge, and in other schools which are actively seeking to redesign their relationships with other schools and in some cases with wider community-based services.
- The dynamic to change the system has to be one that is 'led' rather than 'managed', and risk-taking is an important feature of the role.
- The next steps need to capture the heart of educators and learners, they need to promote widespread debate on the role, function and purpose of schools and they need to be coherent enough to enable people to see how they can be participants in the journey, not mere onlookers watching the show.

NOTES

1   Townsend, Clarke and Ainscow (1999) argue similarly in their recent work.

2   I am fond of W.B. Yeats's saying that 'learning is not about filling buckets but lighting fires in the imagination of the young'.

Chapter 2

Changing the Map: From Schooling to Learning

To cope with a changing world, any entity must develop the capacity of shifting and changing – of developing new skills and attitudes: in short, the capability of learning.
     A. De Gues, *The Living Company*

In the last chapter it was suggested that the emphasis on the type of school that is desired in response to the emergence of the ecological paradigm is changing. The focus of the change is on schools as learning organizations that facilitate learning at personal and organizational levels. This has resulted in a need to reconsider what is happening in present-day school systems and to find ways of making connections between a desired school system and the present one. In part this means that there is a need to challenge the assumptions being made by educators about what is already taking place and to ask whether current reform policy and practice are going to be sufficient in style and scope for the demands of the coming years – and, if they are found wanting, in which direction might they move?

At first glance the argument that schools should be learning organizations appears to be nonsensical. Surely all schools are learning organizations? I suggest that they are not. Schools are still modelled on modern structures which assume hierarchical, sequential, linear and technical understandings of learning which promote instruction and efficiency and excellence, but within a context that will inevitably fail as the new paradigm weighs in. What I believe we need is a new direction established by schools to suit the world that surrounds them. This has to be a direction that is focused on learning and moves away from anachronistic notions of schooling and transmission; in short, the establishment of a learning school within a learning community. These places are more consciously active in seeking connections within and between schools, rather than specialized and singular in their approach to development. They are more integrated places in which to work and study, and are purposefully responsive to meeting the needs of local communities. To achieve this goal, however, there is a need to make transparent the 'expression' (Olds, 1992) of the new learning agenda, and to communicate the ideas and challenges such schools raise in terms that have authenticity and salience with teachers or learners, so as to make the changes that are desired.

To start this chapter I will examine what this thinking looks like. I will then reflect on how the comparisons might influence the work that takes place today in schools and in school support systems.

HOW MIGHT WE CONCEPTUALIZE THE FUTURE SCHOOL?

> How can we find a goal that will allow us to enjoy life while being
> responsible to others?
>   (Csikszentmihalyi, 1997)

I believe we are moving towards a situation where schools operate in the ecological paradigm as places of choice, places of security where it is OK to dream; civilizing places, oases, spiritually nourishing places, places where students and adults focus on things that matter to them and to their deepening understanding of the world and where they collectively explore and deepen that understanding; places which take on important issues and take the high ground rather than seeking the populist solution, places which function as advocates for a better world. In a sense I believe schools should think BIG. They can choose to take the lower ground of 'self-interest with greater gaps between the haves and the have-nots and a continuing deterioration of democracy and the common good' (Fullan, 1999); or they could choose to take a new step along what Fullan calls the 'evolutionary chain' and assume the task of social development, ambitiously taking advantage of their special place in the fabric of society. They should do this from a sound value base that will serve them in the future.

If schools are to rise to these challenges, I believe that they have to look to themselves and how they nurture such qualities amongst all people who work within a school community. There will need to be opportunities for learners, both teachers and students, to make relevant choices and decisions in their own learning and relearning, and this has to be responsive rather than predetermined. It suggests to me that schools should rethink how they exercise choice, power and voice within their institutional make-up.

To be continually challenged in ways that enable the learners to adapt and to apply new working techniques, to be entrepreneurial, and at the same time to establish an awareness as learners that as the work world changes schools and teachers must also change. To accept this argument implies that the established ways of teaching and learning will have to be redesigned because to learn about learning through experience and reflection cannot come from predefined, pre-planned curricula. These lessons come from a real connection with life beyond school, as well as within it, and they come from a responsive and versatile, imaginative set of motivated professionals who can connect such lessons with young people in ways that make sense to them and in ways that expand their present view of reality. What I am suggesting here is that teachers have to be at the vanguard of change and reform, and they have to play an instructive role in creating the types of communities which can themselves learn.

ADAPTING DURING THE LEARNING JOURNEY

A critical component of this learning agenda is the need for adaptivity. Adaptivity demands of the learner the ability to live and learn within challenging situations and to be able to integrate the learning and apply it elsewhere.

21

There is a subtle difference between systems that are *adaptive* from those that are *adapted*. Garmston and Wellman (1995, p. 31) provide an illuminating example from natural history:

> ... there are more than 40 different species of Wildebeests in the parks of South Africa. Wildebeests are specialists, grazing in dry, open spaces. They are willing to migrate long distances in search of such areas. Wildebeests, like other specialists, are more sensitive to environmental changes. And, like other specialists, they are under greater pressure than are generalists. They are adapted through specialisation to specific conditions within tightly defined boundaries. Another significant species in the park lands of Africa is the impala. In Kruger National Park more than 72% of all antelope present are impala. Impalas thrive on a wide variety of vegetation, and can make themselves at home in many different settings. Because of this flexibility, impalas are highly adaptive and change.

Whilst there is a frequent expression of the need for the adaptive learner, it is expected that this learner will come out of an adapted system. This paradox is at the interface of the argument surrounding schooling and learning, a move from a modern to a systemic view. I maintain that we need to design school systems to operate an adaptive model of change and this implies some necessary personal and organizational competences in order to be able to undertake ongoing adaptive responses to changing circumstance.

What might these competences be? They have to promote the types of qualities that an adaptive learner might demonstrate (Townsend, Clarke and Ainscow 1999). The following list serves as an example of adaptive learning competences:

- literacy and numeracy;
- technological capabilities;
- communication skills and exchange of ideas;
- awareness and appreciation of the diversity of human cultures;
- vision and open-mindedness ;
- development capabilities and entrepreneurship;
- critical thinking skills and adaptability;
- teamwork and community service;
- awareness of one's choices;
- commitment to personal and community growth;
- leadership capabilities;
- appreciation of human achievements in the arts and sciences.

ORGANIZATIONAL CHALLENGE

Now we face the challenge. Do our schools already promote these competences? If not, how might they be encouraged, supported and led to enable these competences to be developed? Perhaps crucially, *can* schools promote these competences, do they have the capability to do so, and what do they do? These lines of inquiry lead us to build scenarios, to open up a range of educational possibilities which may or may not happen as a result of our interventions.

Clearly, if schools are to begin to respond to these challenges they are highly likely to need to behave differently in the way they relate to students. There are many definitions of organizations operating as learning places, and one common characteristic of these is changed behaviour (Senge *et al.*, 1994). Changed behaviour comes through common agreement amongst staff that organizational learning has to be a conscious activity, otherwise it operates merely in response to external stimuli in the wider environment. Studies of schools operating as collaborative communities have found that this organizational approach is essential for success (Fullan and Hargreaves, 1992; Louis and Marks, 1996; Steinberg, 1996). More explicitly, Newmann and Wehlage (1995) and Leithwood and Louis (1998) have provided evidence to suggest that there is a powerful relationship between professional community and student performance. These studies indicate that when teachers deliberately pursue together the question of how well their students are doing in their studies, relate this to their teaching strengths and weaknesses and purposefully refine and develop new approaches to modify and improve the quality of what they identify as being significant contributory factors to learner success, the student performance and staff understanding and commitment increase.

I believe that 'conscious choice' (Kegan, 1982) lies at the heart of this issue. It concerns how the school 'thinks' about the matter of educating students. If the school has a predetermined curriculum which it has to 'deliver', it does not have to think about negotiating the process of learning; the learner's voice is immaterial. However, if the education of the student means attempting to put learners in situations where they have to think for themselves, critically challenge and reconstruct ideas, student voice matters and should be taken seriously amongst other significant aspects of organizational attention.

Through its actions a school is therefore publicly indicating how 'conscious' it is of its activity, and the making of choices, as a deliberate and value-driven activity, enables it constantly to take a map reference on its journey. It will identify through specific techniques (which I will outline further, in Chapter 6) what is contributing to and inhibiting its development and it will take steps to overcome these problems through a continuous process of observing, reviewing and adapting. This approach makes some assumptions about change, particularly that it is a dynamic process operating within a living system. Because of this, change does not unfold in a lincar fashion. It frequently causes surprises and creates unpredictable outcomes, it is at the same time personal and collectively felt, and, most importantly, we each have a role to play in it, and by choosing not to take part in an active manner we create an effect just as much as if we actively engage in change events.

THE FOCUSING OF CHOICES TO PROMOTE ADAPTIVITY

Where might the school best focus its choices? It would seem appropriate to focus on those aspects of the work it undertakes as core activity – teaching and learning. From this focus, the school might then be in a position to introduce revised structures in order to achieve core goals of enhanced student performance and deeper staff commitment to and understanding of their teaching.

It is sometimes easier to begin this discussion by focusing on what you might choose to leave behind. Beare (1997) argues that there are some things that you would not have if you were to start again with schools, including:

- the egg-crate classrooms and long corridors;
- the notion of set class groups based on age–grade structures;
- the division of the school day into standard slabs of time;
- the linear curriculum parcelled into step-by-step gradations;
- the parcelling of human knowledge into predetermined boxes called 'subjects';
- the division of staff by subject specialization;
- the allocation of most school tasks to the person called 'teacher';
- the assumption that learning takes place in a place called 'school';
- the artificial walls that barricade school from home and community;
- the notion of a stand-alone school isolated from other schools;
- the notion of a school system bounded by a locality such as a state or even country;
- the limitation of 'formal schooling' to twelve years and between the ages of five and eighteen.
    (Adapted from Beare, 1997, pp. 2–4)

By shaping ideas about what our learning schools should not be, it is also possible to construct an agenda that leads towards establishing something different. These conversations are both a local and system-wide responsibility. While it is not down to every school to reformulate and redesign in totality what they are, neither is it entirely appropriate that such work should be the sole responsibility of government. The task of redefinition and redesign lies, as I have suggested, in the development of learning networks. These might be teacher-led, but they will include other members of the school community, school leaders, teachers and parents, community members from health, social services, and other stakeholders such as government and educational policy-makers at district level.

What might the focus of such schools be? To develop learning materials based on localized interpretations of nationally and globally important themes. There are some important issues that help us to define this agenda further which have been expanded recently in the work of the Royal Society of Arts (RSA) publication *Opening Minds: Education for the 21ˢᵗ Century* (Bayliss, 1999). In this discussion document the RSA suggests a competence framework focusing on five categories that describe what students would achieve as they progress through a curriculum. The RSA competences include:

- learning;
- citizenship;
- relating to people;
- managing situations;
- managing information.

The argument for these competences as a way forward has little to do with the 'failings, real or assumed, of teachers. They are problems of strategy and purpose, and they are not particular to the UK. Across the industrialised world people are struggling to engage with the questions "what should the system look like in twenty years' time and how should it be preparing young people for adult lives?"' (Bayliss, 1999, p.3).

The concerns expressed in the RSA report reflect many of the same concerns voiced by teachers and headteachers when asked about the present curriculum. They concern matters of process, matters of purpose and matters of value. The lack of any credible underpinning philosophy to the national curriculum other than a desire for it to be 'broad and balanced' makes the whole exercise implicit and meaningless, under-debated and, vitally, not shared with or explained to students. This absence of any clarity of purpose underpinning the curriculum results in a lack of meaning and embeddedness into real situations and real lives. Despite good intentions of those who plan and develop it, the curriculum remains for too many a detached and sterile experience rather than a sustained exposure to real challenges and problems. This is a possible reason why teachers often report it as being so difficult, uninspiring and demotivating to teach. As one teacher recently said to me, 'teaching the curriculum that we have at the moment is like training someone as a high-quality chef and then finding that all you are allowed to cook is pizzas in a pizza bar – standard fare, at fair prices, but not exactly "haute cuisine"'.

If we are clear about what it might be that students should learn, then we can also begin to clarify how schools might change their function to provide the appropriate methods to achieve their objectives. If a curriculum were to be focused around some core competences, but how these were to be achieved was to be left to the lead role that teachers should play, then the door swings open for new ways of developing supportive facilities to assist learning at different levels of the system – student, teacher teams, schools and school networks. This raises a couple of points which lie at the very nerve centre of the learning schools theme:

- The development of a school improvement methodology that supports the understanding of change at personal and organizational levels. To proceed with this it is necessary to provide support for schools that can inform them of their present improvement direction, and suggest appropriate interventions to take their activity towards the desired redesign. Here lies the important role of the network as a mediating force, bringing together a collective of people to share successful ways of supporting learners through strategic school activity based around learning.
- The transformation of the education process so that it moves from one of schooling to one of learning. This implies supporting leaders as they promote

activity to develop new ways of using a broader repertoire of learning materials with which to integrate important learning themes into modular programmes in which learners can negotiate their own unique learning pathway. This goal is too big for single schools, and therefore, again, the process relies heavily on localized learning networks which in turn have access to regional, national and international resources to assist in establishing the modular programmes across boundaries.

I believe that serious attention needs to be given to both agendas, and to ways of making them connect meaningfully to establish a curriculum, based on competences, that is transparent, holistic and negotiable rather than prescribed. I believe that if attention is given to both agendas it is possible to develop a very different educational landscape from the one that presently exists, reflecting a different way of thinking about learning and the promotion of learning schools.

Some schools have already started the process of moving from schooling to learning practices. There need not be a dramatic change of direction to move from one paradigm to the other, but there is a need for different ways of thinking about the problem. For example, thinking about learning is often demonstrated in the form of new questions being asked in school about how things are done, why they are done in particular ways, and what might be done to make useful changes to improve upon present activity; reflecting, in short, a change of mindset that seeks to redefine schooling and the purpose of schooling. For instance, there is an increasing necessity for schools to respond to the information they gather on their performance in 'school relevant' ways. The development of diagnostic tools of inquiry that facilitate understanding of the changes being attempted by school is becoming more, not less, important after the external process of inspection of performance has had an impact upon the internal requirement to respond and to take the educational initiative and organizational lead.

School-led inquiry into performance raises the need for ways of thinking about the type of intervention that a school might best undertake, given its identified improvement configuration. This is not a simple issue. It demands a dynamic interpretation of the change configuration that the school might face and cannot be solved just by the simplistic listing of 'key points for action' resulting from an external inspection. Change needs to be understood as a complex issue rather than one that simplifies the matter of educational reform by means of external sources providing 'off-the-shelf' solutions. Whilst the technical solution, seeking simplification of a complex issue, might serve one very specific type of school set of problems, it simply does not fit within a broader transformation of the system. This applies exactly to the situation schools face as they move from old conceptions of 'schooling' to new ones of 'learning'. A paradigm shift from the intelligent but controlling modern mindset of schooling to the creative, interconnected learning mindset of an ecological paradigm (Clarke and Christie, 1997) is a shift in ways of understanding the meaning of improvement. A comparison of some of these changes in educational trends is shown in Table 2.1. Moving from schooling to learning raises the profile of the discussion on what the purpose of schools is; it begins to show us some of the territory into which our learning journey is going to take us as the system transforms from one operational

Table 2.1 *From adapted individualized mindset of schooling to adaptive integrative mindset of learning*

Schooling	Learning
Schools provide formal education programmes which students must attend for a certain minimum amount of time	People have access to learning 24 hours a day, 365 days a year, from a variety of sources, some of which will be schools
Teachers are employed to 'know'. The learner fits in with the teacher	Teachers are employed to match teaching to the needs of the learner
Schools are communities of learners, where individuals are helped to reach their potential	Schools are learning communities where everyone (students, teachers, parents, administrators) is both a learner and a teacher, depending on the circumstances
The information to be learned is graded in a specific way and is learned a particular order. Everyone gets a similar content, with only limited differentiation based on interest	Information is accessed according to the learner's capability and interest. The information will vary greatly after basic skills are learned
Schools are still much the same in form and function as they were when they were first developed	Schools as we know them have been dramatically altered in form and function, or have been replaced
Schools have limited, or no, interactions with those who will employ their students or the people from the community in which the school resides	Communities will be responsible for the education of both students and adults. Business and industry will be actively involved in school developments
Schools are successful if they fit their students into a range of possible futures, from immediate employment as factory hands and unskilled workers to tertiary education for training as professionals	Schools will only be successful if all students have the skills required to work within, and adapt to, a rapidly changing employment, social and economic climate
Formal education institutions are protected from the 'market'	Formal education institutions are subject to 'market' forces, bounded by democratically established local forums

Source: Townsend, Clarke and Ainscow, 1999.

approach to another, from the adapted and individualized to the adaptive and integrated.

If a contrast between the current and future characteristics of schools is made, it is possible to see that there are some underlying concepts about schooling and learning that generate these features. Table 2.2 characterizes recent thinking

Table 2.2 *Schooling and learning: contrasting perspectives*

Individualistic thinking about schooling	Integrative thinking about learning
Important learning can only occur in formal learning facilities	People can learn things from many sources
Everyone must learn a common 'core' of content	Everyone must understand the learning process and have basic learning skills
The learning process is controlled by the teacher. What is to be taught, when it should be taught and how it should be taught are all be determined by a professional person	The learning process is controlled by the learner. What is to be taught, when it should be taught and how it should be taught will all be determined by the learner
Education and learning are individual activities. Success is based on how well learners learn as individuals	Education and learning are highly interactive activities. Success is based on how well learners work together as a team
Formal education prepares people for life	Formal education is the basis for lifelong learning
The terms 'education' and 'school' mean almost the same thing	'School' is only one of a multitude of steps in the education journey
Once you leave formal education, you enter the 'real world'	Formal education provides a range of interactions and networks between learners and the world of politics, economics, spirituality, technology, science and the social
The more formal qualifications you have the more successful you will be	The more capability and adaptability you have the more successful you will be
Basic education is funded by government	Basic education is both funded by government and supported by community and private sources accountable democratically elected to local forums

Source: Townsend, Clarke and Ainscow, 1999.

about the nature and location of learning and compares it with how th
learning might need to change to promote the learning school in t
community.

Reflecting on these comparisons, it is clear that the type of ch
schools face in order to establish the learning school structures sugge
raises considerable challenges, particularly if the school is struggling to s
its present format. These challenges come from a reconceptualization of school
improvement. This will move it away from action that makes tactical changes to
the fabric of the school, based on a false assumption that the basic structure is
fundamentally sound, to one that questions the given assumptions about the
purpose and process of schooling and begins to offer alternatives. The culmina-
tion will be a radical overhaul of the superstructure of schools, taking note of
recent thinking on learning, organizational change and societal changes.

SCHOOL IMPROVEMENT: REDEFINING THE JOURNEY AS A SEARCH FOR DEEPER MEANING

To reconceptualize something demands something more than just changing
behaviour, acquiring specific skills or the mastery of certain preferred types of
knowledge (Kegan, 1994). It makes demands on our minds, how we know, and
how we learn to know. Real educational change will not come about by doing
more of the same things that have been tried before, in the form of refining what
already exists. Real change demands a qualitative difference in how we think
about what we do schools for, and how we go about doing them (Fullan, 1991;
Costa and Garmston, 1994).

One example can be seen in the way that schools fragment learners off into
age-related groups. The result is that little account is taken of the usefulness of
examining different learners' approaches to learning as a result of their different
ages and experience. In effect, schools isolate the learning potential of learners by
designing learning around age-based theories of learner development. The result
of all of this for schools is single-track departments and teaching groups, where
teachers are passionate about their own subject but ignorant of the one taught in
the very next room, which those same learners will have to visit in perhaps 40
minutes' time. No one is considering the demands on learners, the effect on their
sense of what learning actually is, and what meaning their experiences are giving
them about school and particularly about what it means to learn.

The demands schools make on the minds of learners (be they teachers or
students) is therefore a theme in this move towards a new way of thinking about
learning and the role of the school in supporting learning.

CHANGE AND PLANNING: ILLUSIONS OF CERTAINTY IN AN UNCERTAIN WORLD

What is being suggested is that in order to establish a new order of thinking about school improvement, driven by an ecological paradigm of learner and learning, a radical change of ground is needed in the form of method. It is time to think about how schools are to pursue the learning agenda demanded of them if they move from the modern to the ecological paradigm (see Table 2.3).

Table 2.3 *From the modern to the ecological paradigm*

Modern paradigm	Ecological paradigm
mindset of 'managed' change, focused on changing structure by planned reform	mindset of change as 'learning', focused on changing structures and cultures
change as delivery	reflective and critical
implementation-defined	process-defined
visionary	voice
change as simplification of self and organization through clarity of personal role	change as complexification of self and organization through collective investigation of role and organizational purpose
isolationist and individually accountable	collaborative and collectively responsible

Source: Adapted from Clarke and Christie, 1996.

The modern paradigm, the present system, is characterized by the mindset of 'managed' change, where it is often perceived as a set of deliverable events (Mintzberg, 1989). In the modern paradigm it is frequently the advocates of change who make assumptions about the given reality of the school. These assumptions suggest a managerial approach to educational change that accepts the present reality in which schools operate as given and non-negotiable. As a result the activity is to address the technical modifications required to make the present system function in more effective and efficient ways. This interpretation of school needs to have schools themselves as static organizations; in seeing schools in this way the reformers are then able to assume that important conditions exist upon which their reforms will be placed. In some cases this is so, and the changes can be introduced with considerable ease and speed. Invariably such schools are dominated by 'doing' school improvement; they are focused on goals and aim to achieve their goals through a tightly controlled series of delivered changes, according to a schedule that is predefined and led by a vision that suggests that once the planned changes are in place the school will run better, get higher results and achieve greater success. The drivers towards this goal are the teachers, but they operate within individualized agendas rather than undertaking collective activity, and are required to implement changes within set time frames on behalf of the other staff.

The modern paradigm will produce good schools, but at a cost. The cost will be to develop such schools for the wrong era, and they will be full of highly achieving children doing things which are inappropriate for their future lives. The reason for this claim lies in the false assumptions that are being made about education by advocates of effective schooling. They invariably fail to pay sufficient attention to common dynamic features of organizational life, where there may be disputed interpretations of the intended goals or purposes of the change. Where change is contested in any way there will be other observable and unpredictable factors such as the historical legacy of previously introduced reforms, a general lack of consensus on the next steps that should be taken, and the nature of the implementation schedule.

In effect, there has been a considerable overemphasis given to what I will call closed change due to its 'neatness' and certainty, without sufficient attention being given to the open-endedness of many aspects of reform and improvement activity

Table 2.4 *Closed and open-ended change*

Closed change	Open-ended change
Some sequences of events can be recounted clearly	Sequences of events and actions arise from the past and are continuing to affect the future
Why, what and how are commonly agreed	No explanation of events and actions command anything like widespread acceptance by those involved
Starts in the past, develops in the present and moves us into the future. What people do is based on the points of agreement	What people do next to deal with the problem depends on the explanation of past failure that they can agree on – *if they can agree*
Assumes linearity and cause and effect, order, control, stability, consistency and harmony in the local setting of the school	Assumes non-linearity, cause and effect not easily linked

which, by implication, are messy and uncertain (Table 2.4). The consequence of this focus predetermines outcomes and assumes consensus when often the reality of the situation is being cloaked and the open-ended changes are simply being avoided, as they raise too many possible ways of seeing the school.

Closed change also demands visionary leadership so that people know where the change is going and who does what in order to get there. When a change is presented to the recipients of change, it is necessary to suggest that the change will make life that bit easier once it has been introduced. To ensure that everyone agrees to this view, individual accountability is demanded, atomizing the organization.

In contrast, the notion of change as a systemic, ecological paradigm, where all change is seen as integrated, non-linear and initially chaotic, enables all those people involved in the change to search for suitable ways to identify the patterns that they see emerging inside the changes they are observing, to report this to colleagues, and to ensure that they are being heard. This approach assumes a reflective element which draws upon individual and organizational engagement; indeed, it demands such engagement in order to be an informed process. The change is seen as evidence of a complex picture with many layers of impact upon the organization, requiring continual refinement and discussion amongst those whom it affects. It represents both a private and a public community in action.

> Persons are not quite the same as solitary individuals, nor are they a
> crowd. Persons are living networks of biology and emotions and
> memories and relationships. Each is unique, but none can flourish
> alone. Each in some way contains others, and is contained by others,
> without his or her personal truth ever being wholly isolated or
> exhausted. (Tilby, 1989)

Establishing a belief that school can make a difference and that the 'culture' of a school lies within the control of those who participate (Nias *et al.*, 1989) is a notable step in empowering teachers with the language and strategies with which to engage with their action. For schools simply to leave to chance or ignore the open-ended aspects of change because such change is unpredictable and complex (and therefore perhaps unmanageable in the current paradigmatic view) is to rely upon the simplistic belief that external efforts to improve teaching and learning will achieve the desired result. If it were so simple the educational experiment would already be completed.

The very fact that there are influences beyond the education system that affect what is done and how it is done is sufficient to suggest that there is simply too much taking place all around us for us to be in a position to assume that there will be, some time in the future, a 'solved' problem to the matter of education and learning. Schein (1992) forcefully argues this when he says that we must build on the assumption that the world is intrinsically complex, non-linear and over-determined. We have to learn that because of its complexity the problem is very difficult to predict, but efforts to make more sense of it, to 'discover one's own mental models, and to test those against discovered reality constitute a valuable process that improves one's ability to cope' (Schein, 1992, p. 372).

The next chapter will make a case for reconceptualizing school improvement so that it is undertaking activity that serves learning school agendas, and not those failed approaches derived from the modernistic principles of schooling.

KEY ISSUES AND IDEAS IN THIS CHAPTER

- Schools will play a leading role in the redefinition of the system as it moves from schooling to learning.
- This role demands that they make choices, or, if not, choices will be made for them. These choices should be embedded within a system-wide debate about how they can contribute to the greater good of society.
- There are demanding new competences that schools need to facilitate as they create a culture of adaptivity in learning. The core capabilities lie in the ability to pursue learning at an individual and at a collective level.
- These competences demand a rethinking of the way school improvement is undertaken so that it more proactively transforms the school agenda towards learning rather than persistently responding and attempting to modify present conditions for the management of schooling. This needs to address an understanding of the personal and the collective/organizational learning strengths and needs.
- To achieve a transformation of this type it is necessary to try to develop a dynamic model of school change so that the complexity lived out on a daily basis in schools is acknowledged and used constructively to inform an ongoing investigation into the learning process.
- This model has to account for points of agreement as well as points that are contested, and these points will in turn be both personally and collectively contested.
- The effort to develop a new model of improvement is to enhance the ability of people to cope with the sheer immensity of change and in doing so, to begin to 're-normalize' their organizational reality against the emerging redesigned system.

Chapter 3

Moving from Part to Whole: From the Instrumental to the Sustainable

I know of no safe depository of the ultimate powers of the society but the people themselves; and if we think them not to be enlightened enough to exercise their control with a wholesome discretion, the remedy is not to take it from them but to inform their discretion.
Thomas Jefferson, Letter to Charles Jarvis, 28 September 1820

In the last chapter I suggested that choice is an important indicator of a learning school. The process of identification of the right path to choose is difficult, as it demands an organizational awareness of the implications of the data sets that it draws upon, and an awareness of the repertoire of possible processes that it can use to make the activity a collaborative one rather than a fragmented exercise. Choice brings together the form and function of the improvement activity, and attention needs to be paid to both. Choices that become adopted into functional improvement plans indicate how schools presently see their improvement work and demonstrate publicly their perception of organizational reality, they are necessary but they are not on their own sufficient to create transformations from schooling to learning. The form of the plans matters too. What type of improvement do schools seek, and, on whose terms do they seek it? The problem that our schools face concerns how much choice they feel they are able to exercise over issues that really matter. If they are unable to exercise their discretion in areas of importance they will end up falling into the role of technicians accommodating changes for someone else's agenda. l suggest in this chapter that there are some problems with the ways that this organizational reality is understood as it is played out in what we have come to call school improvement. These problems are constrained by a cultural preference for economic growth and development as the basis for educational reform, rather than change, which is intricately linked with thinking about the underlying purpose of education.

Central to this argument is the view that current reform is driven by the misconception that structural changes will be sufficient to enhance organizational performance. Instead, a case is made for reconceptualizing school improvement so that it serves learning school agendas, not modernistic approaches which seek cultural reform and primarily seek conceptual change about learning and the purpose of schools. This discussion will lead me to be able to ask the questions that drive the second part of the book: How can schools learn? And if they can, what can they be helped to learn which will illuminate present ways of working and provide insight that can introduce new and sustainable practices in the future?[1]

FIRST STEPS: FROM CONSENSUS TO CONTEST

One persistent message of this book is that we stop taking for granted what we currently accept as the correct way to improve schools. I believe that many of the approaches that are being presented to schools as the right way to improve do not equip them in practice or structure for a changing world. The present way of approaching the improvement of schools is not characterized by strategy that seeks to problematize the need for change. Instead, it is a way of seeing improvement as a series of planned, implemented and scheduled activities.

In this chapter I will suggest that 'seeing' successful school improvement as the ability to live with contested and problematic issues is a more realistic and developmentally helpful way of preparing for sustained reform. This way of operating implies an acceptance that *conflict* is a necessary dynamic of good reform and a healthy, learning environment.

But this understanding does not come easily. The ability to live in a climate that uses conflict constructively to focus and facilitate new understanding about what is working and what is not working demands an environment that can accept different and often conflicting positions on the same issue without producing personal and collective turmoil. It requires a different kind of concept of the improvement agenda as one that is about building ever stronger bonds between teams who are all engaged in the learning process.

At present, the common-sense viewpoint is to argue for the opposite and to suggest that harmony and consensus lead to successful change and are organizational prerequisites. But collective thoughts and knowledge about 'what schools are' and 'what schools should be' are often so automated (Bohm, 1992) that we have in large part become controlled by them, with a subsequent loss of localized authenticity and purpose, freedom and meaning. The conscious awareness of different ideas and approaches to the same issue moves us out of our consensual slumbers and awakens us to the possibility of difference as an instrument of renewal.

Given what I have just said, it is therefore perhaps appropriate that the actions currently being promoted for the development of the school are critically challenged. The current improvement skill base is driven by simplistic notions of change, simplified interpretations of what is a complex weave of social, emotional and cultural learning, and an overdependence on management activity rather than on teaching and learning. It needs reconceptualizing, taking schools away from instrumentalism and individualization of school and learner for the purpose of economic gain, towards a more networked, interconnected and mutually sustainable learning agenda.

Conflicting ideas

Beare *et al.* (1994) suggest that ideas exist in tension and can be expressed as views that are in decline competing with views that are in ascendancy. Competing views of the role and purpose of schools are currently experienced as tensions as they play themselves out through institutional as well as personal approaches to the day-to-day job of teaching. What was once the most appropriate way to work with learners might now no longer be considered to be so effective, as a result of a change in the way that the thinking and the practice of supporting learning move from one conceptual approach to another. The ideas in decline command considerable status as the defining reality for the institutions we work in because they reflect what the institution once was, whereas ideas in ascendency tend to be less defined, more vulnerable and likely to be contested and open-ended in their interpretation.

An example of how ideas in decline and ideas in ascendency influence school activity can be seen in the changes taking place in the global society, as developed countries move from industrial into post-industrial information-enriched working. Our understandings of both these worlds overlap. What was once cherished, complete, trusted, contained and localized within single institutions is beginning to be questioned and challenged as the paradigmatic coherence becomes less stable. Often, as seen at the school level, we hold on to the values and beliefs of one age as we struggle to understand the new one. In such situations, the maturity of the institution can play a significant part in restricting the capacity to respond to change. Schools have learnt to develop a set of operational approaches to reform which suit the conditions and expectations of their interpretation of the problems they face. These remain workable as long as their interpretation of the conditions and expectations is valid. If their interpretation is flawed because it fails to illuminate aspects of organizational life that are being taken for granted, they are likely to experience increasing organizational turbulence.

These interpretations of present reality through 'past' viewpoints are responses which have no future but which would have been effective in the past; they are Baudrillards' (1994) 'fossils'. As a consequence, the core beliefs and values that apply to the old paradigm obscure and confuse the organization about what it means to be part of the new.

> The choice between competing paradigms proves to be a choice
> between incompatible modes of community life when paradigms
> enter, as they must, into a debate about paradigm choice, their role is
> necessarily circular. Each group uses its own paradigm to argue in
> that paradigm's defence. The resulting circularity does not, of course,
> make the arguments wrong or even ineffectual. Yet whatever its
> force, the status of the argument is only that of persuasion. It cannot
> be made logically or even probabilistically compelling for those who
> refuse to step into the circle. The premises and values are not
> sufficiently extensive for that. As in political revolutions, so in
> paradigm choice. There is no standard higher than the assent of the
> relevant community. (Kuhn, 1970, p. 94)

As Kuhn suggests, any changes that are introduced into any setting will be contested and accorded to the mindset of either the old or the new. Just as at a global level we can see that nineteenth-century imperialism has gradually been replaced by twentieth-century economic imperialism, our education systems seem determined to deliver an education to youngsters in readiness for a world which no longer exists (Stoll and Fink, 1996). The values and beliefs that constitute the world view of an industrial society, reflected in its educational priorities, may be in decline, and their manifestations in most of the developed world have generally run their course. As Orr (1994) suggests, this remains problematic if we are to seek alternatives that might offer more appropriate directions for education and learning in the future:

> ... as Homo Sapiens's entry into any intergalactic design competition, industrial civilisation would be tossed out at the qualifying round ... The design failures of industrially/technologically driven societies are manifest in the loss of diversity of all kinds ... pollution, soil erosion, ugliness, poverty, injustice, social decay, and economic instability. (Orr, 1994, p. 104)

Orr is suggesting that the inheritance of this dominant way of doing things for 150 years is still all around us but is now seriously in decline, the current and most obvious emphasis being one of economic and social progress. In first-world countries, where economic and political structures of global and national development continue to be very powerful and where their dynamism and resilience help to explain their success, its main features include increased material affluence, advances in health care and technological innovation.

> ... but perhaps even more powerful is the conceptual framework underlying and informing the structures. The dominant intellectual model of economic and social progress has had an extraordinary grip not just on politicians, economists and policy makers but, in turn, on the mental pictures of the general public. It has governed our understanding both of the objectives of 'development' and of the mechanisms required to achieve it. (Orr, 1994)

The first world's modern industrial world view has evolved into 'globalization': we move from one set of technologies to another, from one set of issues to another, and we identify problems about how best to manage human life on a crowded planet. The underlying problems of this world are emerging in sufficient volume and frequency to challenge the dominant paradigm and demand different solutions to those of the old order. This could be explained as a result of the old order's success in globalizing issues which were previously understood only at a local level, such as the need to feed, employ, communicate and establish a social harmony for collective benefit. As globalization has developed and been appropriated since the mid-1960s through corporate business and telecommunications, it has changed the notion of national and international trading barriers and influenced national and transnational discourses on how to live and work (Saul, 1998).

Schools and school systems in the West continue to carry conceptions of schooling which reflect the preoccupations of their local rather than their international histories. We can see evidence of this phenomenon in both their structures and their customs. As Schlechty (1990) has observed 'to get one's business right one must consider what purposes the enterprise has served in the past, as well as the purposes the enterprise could serve in the future'. For example, the architecture of the old triple-decker 'workhouse-like' Victorian schools still evident in London and many of the cotton-belt cities in the north of England, as well as their smaller siblings in many villages, display many of the design features of an industrial age and provide continuing symbols of their foundations.

Further evidence of the past operating in the present school system is illustrated by Schlechty (1990) in metaphors of the changing functions of the school:

- School as community church, promoting morality and civic good, reverence for school, teaching as a sacred profession;
- School as factory, whose purpose was economic, selection grading and standardization, managed by principles derived from a view of the organization as a machine, teachers as skilled technocrats;
- School as hospital, to ameliorate injustices of industrial society, children seen as clients, and curriculum individualized.

Schools today carry aspects of all three functions, despite the contradictions and tensions which the varying functions bring. They are now also being asked to face a future function, which Schlechty describes without metaphor:

- School as a knowledge–work organization, to help students learn what they need to know in a knowledge–work world; curriculum becomes a body of knowledge to be processed and formed by students who are workers and customers.

If we are to begin to reclaim some territory from this colonization by economic necessities of a modern paradigm we would have to see change. The school as a knowledge–work organization helps students to emerge as transformers of their own lives. They could, in principle, achieve this inside the modern paradigm. However, if we are to make the shift to an ecological paradigm, in my view an essential shift for the integrative system to flourish, it is imperative that the students, as well as the staff experience something of the collective, co-operative benefit of working, seeing and living differently inside a network of learning schools. In this network the community of the school as a community of learners reclaims the learning territory for itself, and then recycles the skills to do this with other colleagues inside the wider network. The role played by teachers and all those engaged in the community of the school is that of participants in redefining the meaning of the school as a learning community, where school improvement is seen as part of an emancipatory discourse (Fairclough, 1989).

CROSSING BORDERS: THE DISPUTED TERRITORY BETWEEN MAINTENANCE AND DEVELOPMENT

My next theme argues that school improvement should be more deliberately considering the future and being proactive in change, rather than responding to it. The reason is that the dominant individualistic view assumes power over others through hierarchy. In order to improve the system it becomes necessary to simplify, not complicate, the improvement process and to play a role of maintenance rather than development, avoiding the destabilizing force of risk of failure (Clarke and Christie, 1997).

I have argued elsewhere (Clarke, 1996) that an instrumental approach to improvement is unlikely to produce sustainable changes in schools as there is little need for reflective activity in a view of learning that instructs teachers on what to do. Literacy hours under the present curriculum reforms illustrate this in their overprescription of technicality. Successful schools operating in an individualistic system will buy their performance at the expense of other local schools, which will sink as a result. A headteacher told me recently in all seriousness that his Key Stage 1 results would improve this year because he was able to 'buy a top teacher from down the road'. No doubt he thinks his school will improve. However, his remark says something about the system in which the school is operating. All schools suffer and 'get better at a bad game' (Fullan, 1993) if they continue to pursue such approaches. In soccer there is room for only one Manchester United, in education we cannot afford losers; the social and economic costs are simply too high.

But there is a further and more fundamental danger from instrumentalism. It relates to the purposes of school improvement and of education itself. What view of the future and the purpose of education are we trying to realize through these improvement initiatives and processes? What are the dangers of considering education as a commodity , and of the view of the world as a supermarket where democracy's highest manifestation is consumption? A recent report to UNESCO on education for the twenty-first century drew attention to this grotesque distortion of education:

> Education has other purposes than to provide a skilled workforce for
> the economy: it should serve to make human beings not the means
> but the justification of development. (UNESCO, 1996, p. 80)

I have suggested that schools exist in a changing rather than fixed global context, and that the burdens of their histories are not allowing them to cope with the present changes that the global arena places on them, let alone enabling them to be actively shaping their future. Recent conceptions of the world as a machine are being replaced in many disciplines by a more systemic view, for example in new physics, biology, psychology, mathematics and ecological studies (Capra, 1996). The underlying similarity of these different subjects lies in the search for a more interconnected understanding of our complex world. The implications are not lost on organizations such as schools and on thinking about how we might model schools as learning centres, and wedded to this issue is the question of how to proceed with school improvement so that it remains relevant and challenging rather than reactive and predictable. This thinking has, of course, been applied to promoting change in education systems (see for example Fullan, 1991; Sarason, 1990) but has not been taken on in a connected way by policy-makers; rather, we see selected parcels of simulation which appear radical but remain safely inside the current paradigm (Thompson, 1999; DfEE, 1998). For example, Fullan's recommendation to combine pressure and support has been embraced in the new Labour Government's education policy. Treating problems as 'friends' (Fullan, 1993) has not. As Mickelthwait and Woolridge, cited in Hargreaves and Fullan (1998, p. 131) suggest:

> First . . . the state is an incredibly blunt instrument; it gets hold of one overarching idea and imposes it without any sensitivity on the local context . . . second is the desperate craving of politicians for a magical solution.

If school improvement allies itself with the dominant discourse in education then it will have little of the transformative power of critical function. This is reflected in the view

> . . . that knowledge, power and technique are of primary significance and should therefore dictate the path to the future . . . What matters are the practical arrangements for getting things done. Here we see the foundations of Dystopia, the machine-led view of the future which leads inexorably to a world unfit for life (Slaughter, 1994, p. 26–7).

We see evidence of an instrumental improvement approach being taken to pursue initiatives such as target setting, literacy and numeracy hours, and the 'naming' and 'shaming' of schools. These have all been supported by central government to improve school performance. As Slaughter's 'practical arrangements' (1994), these strategies demonstrate:

- **Shallowness**: defines success as a narrow range of outputs such as the proportion of pupils attaining higher grades in five GCSE subjects, which do not reflect the more complex and human purposes of schooling;
- **Fundamentalism**: prescribes strategies based on unquestioned beliefs and dogmas and not on knowledge, research or values which cherish people (for example, naming and shaming);
- **Decontextualization**: holds schools to account for the outputs of an organization when they have very little control over the inputs;
- **Selection**: ignores important aspects of children's development, especially the social aspects, and future citizenship, and areas of knowledge outside the prescribed content of the National Curriculum;
- **Exclusiveness**: focuses on a narrow range of students (borderline C/D grades at GCSE) or is dependent on technology, or on a narrow range of teaching styles such as the 'chalk and talk, drill and recite' mode of teaching, which still dominates the repertoire of most teachers despite its poor track record. (Joyce, Calhoun, and Hopkins, 1997)

As strategies these are ultimately unlikely to produce sustained improvements because they fail to address some important aspects of what it means to be 'at school'. They do not, for example, allow learners to explore their learning through both the content and the form of what they learn, or to examine what it means to be a human in our school system as adults working under intensified conditions (Apple, 1983), or as young learners exploring their development as social, physical, political, beings engaging in activity that establishes their own foundations for their future lives. Harnessing schools to the national economic project supersedes all these considerations. The Bishop of Ripon made this point forcibly in a debate in the House of Lords on 2 February 1994:

'Learning to Succeed.' Yes, but for what? I understand the need for economic growth but, as a goal in itself, surely it stands as barren and arid? Education stands in danger of seeing people only as tools for economic progress, unless it is accompanied by a vision of individuals as creative, responsible and spiritual and society as the matrix within which genuine fulfilment is the goal for all. 'No time to waste', says the National Commission on Education report, and I endorse that sentiment. But I would add to it another one: 'No people to waste,' I believe that at this moment our society is in danger of wasting people. (Young, 1994)

The continuing hold of the instrumentalist view can in part be put down to the understandable imperative for policy-makers and politicians to demonstrate that they are making a difference. Whilst this is of interest and importance, it is only a part of the wider sphere of thinking that the learning school must colonize.

STEPPING INTO THE NEW TERRITORY: LEAVING BEHIND THE OLD ARGUMENTS

The uncertainty of our future, linked with the drive for certainty and stability of our present organizational mindsets in schools and supporting school systems, means that we face a turbulent and paradoxical moment in school evolution. We must, to put it simply, dare to take the next step, trust in the creative ability of colleagues and step into a different conceptualization of schools, one which departs from some of the old ways of schooling students into one which informs, educates and challenges the perspectives on learning that presume certainty and absolutes in favour of creative responses to the challenges of life, learning and living.

In tackling these aspects of the improvement agenda I suggest we need to reconsider the themes I have raised and place them into a debate about what an alternative model for improvement might pursue and be built around. To move into this territory we might reconsider:

- How schools are encouraged to change;
- The ideas in decline and those in ascendency that influence and define the improvement paradigm;
- How to change the emphasis from maintenance and management of isolated schools to the development of a learning system.

These issues have been chosen because they illustrate the hidden dynamics of the agenda that must be confronted in order to move school improvement from the modern to the ecological paradigm outlined in Chapter 2 (see Table 2.3).

How schools are told to change

Change has become an enduring feature of school life, despite the continued efforts of policy-makers to argue that they will establish conditions of stability (DfEE, 1998). What for some is described as 'modernization', for others, however, seems to indicate a revisionist and reductionist agenda that serves policy-makers and politicians rather than ringing with localized purpose and meaning. In his analysis of the failings of the 'quality circle' often used to inform the process of educational reform, Pring (1998) reported a sequence of assumptions being made about how schools should define, develop and manage change.

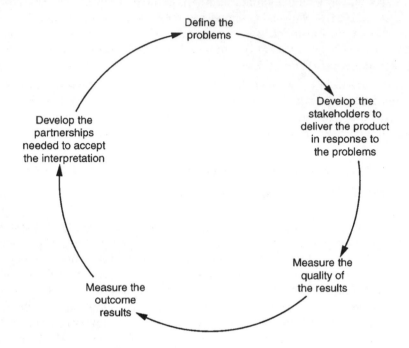

Figure 3.1 *Quality circle for improvement*

This management of reform and improvement is a feature embedded in most English schools' method of planning and responding to changing practice. While on the surface it offers a certainty of meeting expectations and indicating a 'proper' approach to change, it is essentially a deeply conservative and reactionary way of changing school. As a method, it fails completely to offer anything other than the maintenance of the status quo, because there is no critical questioning demanded of the nature and purpose of the change itself. The result of this approach to the process of school improvement has been to contain the improvement agenda within a paradigm dominated by modernistic notions of control, authority and management. A central feature of this paradigm is the idea that a series of inputs and outputs will, when linked in the correct ways, result in a better school or school system. The results of this way of approaching educational reform are very obvious. It becomes a necessity to predefine the curriculum so that there is a base from which to measure the impact of the attempts to introduce changes (Summers and Johnson, 1996). It becomes a necessity to define what teachers can and cannot do in the name of teaching, it becomes a necessity to define the ways that headteachers should manage their schools, and it becomes a necessity to define 'leadership' so that the 'right' types of leaders take forward the 'right' types of changes.

The quality circle approach has attraction at a policy level. It allows people outside the direct activity of the institution of the school to begin to make what they believe are legitimate choices on behalf of learners. For example, if curriculum content can be externally defined, then there should also be defined ways in which that curriculum is 'delivered' by teachers to learners so as to assure quality of provision. This delivery has to be 'value-free' (Woodhead, 1998) untainted by the ideological idiosyncrasies of personality on the basis of making the system equitable for all users irrespective of location, otherwise consistency of quality cannot be controlled.

Similarly, it becomes imperative that those people who are promoted to the role of managing the schools must co-operate and actively endorse the approaches being espoused 'beyond the school' and act as advocates of it, otherwise the impact of the approach is severely hampered. Therefore we witness the development of state-validated 'leadership' and 'headteacher training' requirements, to minimize the risk of maverick leaders and managers who would inhibit the activity of the state upon the school system.

Argyris (1990) suggests that such approaches are evidence of what he calls 'skilled incompetence'. The main characteristics emerge when human beings are put into situations where they believe they have to act in ways that indicate publicly that they are in control. These actions are well established in social settings, as we are taught them early in life, especially 'when people are dealing with issues that can be embarrassing or threatening'. They include ways of dealing with challenging situations, as they contain rules that are used to define, design and be implemented in our organizational day-to-day lives. Changing schools is one example: people will often not confront the embarrassment of saying what they really believe for fear of creating a scene or establishing an atmosphere of unease and tension. Argyris goes on to suggest that these actions are an example of the 'playing out' of individual and collective theories of how to work together. They contain a defensive reasoning used to legitimize failing approaches. This reasoning produces unintended consequences in people do not say what they really want to say, but instead 'stew' in their silence. Because this is a trained skill, honed through years of avoidance of conflict, disharmony and challenge to established values and principles, we find real change difficult to establish and to introduce in the form of activity which will have any substantial effect on the well-established culture of school. In many cases we are not even aware that we are creating these unintended consequences, nor are we aware of the hidden dynamics they promote.

The hidden dynamics of improvement activity, then, can be summarized as:

- **Avoidance**: A use of success to cover failures, leading to:
- **Superficiality**: Avoidance by people at all levels of the system (senior policy-makers, administrators, teachers and managers) of the fundamental causes of the problems facing schools, so that their efforts are increasingly superficial in nature and they maintain and legitimize the development of organizational barriers to real improvement.

- **Consequence**: A recognition that the attempts to improve one aspect of school performance often have unintended and catastrophic consequences elsewhere.

In the example of the literacy hour (see box) we see how the use of success to avoid discussing problems and failure creates a situation where the improvement discourse is reduced to superficial matters and fails to get to the significant matter: how to create a more constructive and trusting environment in which staff feel able to have a meaningful voice in the change process. There are a number of consequences for the way management functions within the present modern improvement paradigm, which in turn provide fertile ground for those interested in establishing an alternative vision of the future to present contrasting view-points. It is a matter of debate whether these consequences are intended or unintended, as many of the unintended consequences could easily be aligned to purposeful political activity. However, establishing contrasts serves as a device to illustrate the point (see Table 3.1).

The literacy hour - a story of consequences

In a recent meeting of staff a headteacher reported what she saw as the usefulness of the literacy hour in her school. She spoke of how the materials had been shared, how they had been applied consistently, how the approach had been agreed amongst staff and how positive the staff were about the resource, suggesting that it had provided a sense of clarity, direction and structure to the teachers' work.

When the teaching staff were questioned after the meeting about their view of the introduction of the literacy hour, a very different picture emerged. Teaching staff said that it had been presented to them as a non-negotiable activity and that they had had no opportunity in formal meetings to raise any concerns about the process. They said that the meetings they had attended in school to discuss the literacy hour had resulted in the headteacher refusing to deviate from the presented hour-long formula, arguing that it was statutory when in fact it was not. Staff said that when they had asked individually to discuss the matter further with the headteacher she suggested that they were making trouble and that there had been consensus at the staff meetings when it had been raised. They said that their intentions had been to explore ways of modifying and integrating to already successful approaches, but this was refused because it implied inconsistency. To enforce the standard approach, the headteacher stated her intention to undertake spot checks on teachers in class.

The intended introduction of the reform resulted in a half-hearted and technical response from staff who are teaching the literacy hour, with little enthusiasm or energy. The subsequent effect on the staff as a whole has been one of demoralization, threatening the impending introduction of the numeracy hour. The staff seldom question, engage in innovation with enthusiasm or raise issues that are of school-wide concern. Instead, they have adopted the appearance of compliance, but beyond the whole school meetings they report personal fears, anxiety and disillusion about the direction in which the school is moving.

Table 3.1. *Intended and unintended consequences of policy*

Intended consequences	Unintended consequences
To develop a system where the accountability of the school is driven by what can be observed and reported upon	Anything unobservable must be regarded as suspect
To pursue a policy that drives for ever more reliable and measurable data	Teaching staff are driven to provide technical evidence in the form of outcomes and predictions An objective reality is inferred that detracts from the legitimacy of the personal view
To avoid open-ended questions not capable of being empirically tested	Any learning that is unplanned is to be avoided because it will raise the threshold of doubt and uncertainty

Improvement, measurement and resistance to change

To develop a system where the accountability of the school is driven by what can be observed and reported upon leads to a situation where anything unobservable has to be regarded as suspect, and this includes what teachers do with learners. It is therefore necessary to make teachers as accountable as possible, inside each school, to their part in the delivery of the curriculum programme, so that any deviance from it or failure to get learners through it prompts immediate action first by colleagues, and in the second instance by external checks.

In order to maintain monitoring of the activity of the school, and to ensure compliance, it is necessary to enhance the status and the profile of the most observable and measurable features of school activity. These closely correlate to the curriculum packages and in turn, these packages necessarily demand technical competences of teachers to apply them in the desired manner. A second effect is that an objective reality is inferred as a result of the pursuit of hard data, which has negative effects on the teacher's interpretation of what is happening in school and makes that teacher's view less potent, powerful and legitimate in its influence (Carr and Kemmis, 1986).

Let me give you an example of this. I was asked to talk to a large group of primary headteachers at an LEA conference. During the morning, the headteachers were given a series of inputs from advisers and then from a headteacher. The headteacher was well known in the LEA and gave an entertaining and practical talk on how he had made changes to the way his school worked, and then led on to some generalizations about things for others to look out for. During his talk, and during the LEA adviser's talk, persistent messages were being given about the importance they attached to the idea that this day should have immediate bearing on what headteachers did on the following working day in school. Indeed, the headteacher openly stated that if the day didn't give a 'bucketload of answers' it would not be worth spending time there. This underlying message troubled me, not just because I had no intention of giving 'bucketloads of answers' but because I felt that it was fundamentally the wrong type of message to be suggesting. It seemed to me that it endorsed an approach to the improvement of schools that amplified avoidance, superficiality and simplistic cause-and-effect thinking at the expense of critical reflection on the variation of contexts within which other schools might be working. Equally revealing, was the evaluation process which concluded this day, a process that now seems to be a prevalent means of measuring impact for such days; it asked delegates to register on a scale of 1 to 5 (1 being highest, 5 lowest) their view of the day in terms of its 'immediate practical use'. Nowhere was there any indication of evaluative activity which indicated integrated thinking, the development of new ideas, anything suggesting that the themes were coherent or able to foster a series of new questions at school or intra-school level. This superficiality left me feeling very uneasy about what I had been asked to do (and in no doubt what I had done was unsatisfactory in the eyes of the receivers as well as the planners!)

This experience caused me to think about what the process of school improvement had evolved into. What was being contested, and what I believe demonstrates a common feature of school improvement operating inside the modern paradigm in which schools are currently operating, was a matter of differing views of what counts as knowledge within organizational culture. Here is Joseph Schwab (1964, p. 14):

> The dependence of knowledge on a conceptual structure means that any body of knowledge is likely to be of only temporary significance. For the knowledge which develops from the use of a given concept usually discloses new complexities of the subject matter which call forth new concepts. These new concepts in turn give rise to new bodies of enquiry and, therefore, to new and more complete bodies of knowledge stated in new terms.

I believe that in recent times a 'cherry-picked' school improvement literature has been accommodated into the old order, prioritizing maintenance arguments; it has become mainstream and in doing so it has lost most if not all of its potential emancipatory edge.

Over the past fifteen or so years, the effectiveness and improvement literature has been highly influential on the ways in which governments have encouraged schools to develop. This research and the subsequent literature have evolved, and yet as new complexities are disclosed the literature becomes increasingly mis-represented and it is more difficult to raise counter-arguments for improvement because the concepts that are emerging and in ascendancy illuminate the tempo-rary nature of much of the earlier material. Problems arise because the old material provides the present bedrock of school reality; many careers are at stake in maintaining and promoting material of the old order. The more it dates, the greater the need for control, and so the material becomes reduced to a series of seemingly unchallengable assumptions on how schools should function, cham-pioned by a powerful elite. These assumptions are used to validate the activity of schools, and through these refined, technicized and sterile versions of school improvement efforts schools, teachers and students have succeeded in marginalizing the debate about the improvement of schools within a social context and thus in generalizing individual school reform agendas in a desperate effort to maintain the management of schooling under the modern paradigm. Therefore schools, teachers and students face superficiality, avoidance and the consequent accusation of failure if they pursue anything other than the mandated approach.

Fortunately, learning remains complex and for the most part involves the close personal and emotional link between the teacher and the learner (Ainscow and Southworth, 1996; Connell *et al.*, 1995). If in the improvement of the school canon it is decided that we should ignore and marginalize complex questions as not capable of testing and decide, by stealth or through deliberate ignorance, that they are to be avoided because they will raise the spectre of doubt and uncertainty, both of which are to be eradicated from a modernization programme, we will take school improvement nowhere and we will be colluding in the 'dumbing down' of education – a consequence of which is to inhibit, rather then liberate, new thinking on how to support learning other than that which is pre-planned.

While these implications of an effective 'schooling' reform agenda prevail, they also have other less overt effects. These include the need to belittle any feature of educational discourse which raises speculation from perspectives other than the mainstream. In particular it becomes necessary to deny the importance of the learner, in terms of the integrity of the learner as a unique individual, and any learning that this learner might bring to the school that lies outside of the orthodox curriculum. The selective reading of the effective schooling literature is an example of how politically expedient features can distort what was once a radical agenda for change. The drive to accommodate within the educational paradigm only that which is seen, and to do so in some 'value-free' manner devoid of the human viewpoint rapidly transforms school improvement into an exercise in sterile, safe, dehumanized, decontaminated reform, where teachers are the technical accomplices to an unknown educational mechanic.

The present approaches used in school improvement address the system from the perspective that everything is basically sound and that, with some minor alterations to optimise the system, all will be solved (Mkhatshwa, 1998; Mintzberg, 1994). This assumes that the model is correct, and yet we know that considerable changes are taking place within local and global societies and that these influence and modify the way we respond in dramatic and unpredictable ways. School improvement that operates within this restrictive, minor modification approach is not going to make links between the present context and those discussions that are taking place about the future role of schools.

JOURNEYING INTO THE IMPOSSIBLE

'I can't believe that!' said Alice, ' . . . one can't believe impossible
things.' 'I daresay you haven't had much practice,' said the Queen.
'When I was your age, I always did it for half-an-hour a day. Why,
sometimes I've believed as many as six impossible thiings before
breakfast.' (Lewis Carroll, *Through the Looking Glass*)

I felt it important to contextualize the improvement agenda into the present paradigmatic frame because it enables me now to try and provide starting points for the reconceptualization of the improvement agenda and bring together the two competing paradigmatic agendas operating in dynamic tension. This represents what Zohar and Marshall (1993) describe as 'learning to think the impossible'. We can see that the social patterns that evolve inside our schools, together with the institutional structures that we adopt, serve to structure our ideas about what is possible and appropriate in any reform. These patterns of thinking are personal and collective and they hold us inside ways of seeing that are immensely powerful and influential.

To change schools, therefore, means that we have to change the ways we think about them (Bohm, 1992). We need to develop a new language of improvement that is better designed to respond to the problems of the present and lead into the future, rather than one that is designed around the solution of problems belonging to an age gone by. The predominant ways of thinking draw from the Newtonian age (Wheatley, 1994); where categories of time, movement and cause-and-effect relationships, framed how people came to see the world around them. Whereas the legacy of much of the improvement literature has been to focus on conditions, less is said about the direction in which the school might focus its teaching and learning attention as it evolves and improves in its organizational activity. I feel that we need to develop the ability to speak of the 'impossible things' of Lewis Carroll's White Queen and reinstate some emancipatory zeal into the improvement debate.

The problem is not that we can't do it, but that we have grown so accustomed to seeing the world through common-sense notions of time, measurement, cause and effect that other ways seem impossible. I shall revisit here the RSA material from Chapter 2 (Bayliss, 1999), as I believe it provides some useful insights into the type of territory that the school might usefully explore in redesigning its curriculum for the future – making the impossible possible by connecting the experience of the school closely with the experiences and challenges the wider world will provide when students leave school.

- Learning about learning – teaching students skills that enable them to select relevant techniques to help them to learn, and to retain and recall understanding and knowledge;
- Citizenship – the important role and responsibilities that they have as participants in a wider society;
- Relating to people – the types of competence that they need in order to establish and maintain genuine and satisfactory relationships with other people;
- Managing situations – providing students with opportunities to experience and reflect on how to interpret and tackle situations and to communicate purposefully and with sensitivity to others' needs;
- Managing information – enabling students to understand, use and apply information which they can draw from a variety of sources.

I shall also revisit the themes identified as being salient for the 'third millennial school', as these promote some of the new challenges schools face (Townsend, Clarke and Ainscow, 1999):

- People have access to learning 24 hours a day, 365 days a year, through a variety of sources, some of which will be schools.
- Teachers are employed to match teaching to the needs of the learner.
- Schools are learning communities where everyone (students, teachers, parents, administrators) is both a learner and a teacher, depending on the circumstances.
- Information is accessed according to the learner's capability and interest. The information will vary greatly after basic skills are learned.
- Schools as we know them have been dramatically altered in form and function, or have been replaced.
- Communities will be responsible for the education of both students and adults. Business and industry will be actively involved in school developments.
- Schools will only be successful if all students have the skills required to work within, and adapt to, a rapidly changing employment, social and economic climate.
- Formal education institutions are subject to 'market' forces bounded by democratically established local forums.

How might we begin to express and achieve this agenda? Quite simply, by integrating arguments, bringing together the network of ideas that exist to facilitate a new form of seeing. In searching for this new language for learning we can learn a lot from new science. The beauty of quantum physics, complexity theory and ecological research is in their illustrative manner, in which it becomes possible to see impossible things that are evident everywhere around us at all times and yet are rarely seen and felt because we simply don't look in that way. Our particular expectations of the mechanistic view of the world have resulted in our expecting certain things from the world we observe. We look for what we expect to see. Newtonian physics tells us to expect that when we push something it will move in the desired direction. We perceive our institutions as separate entities, linked through sequences of power and command. One set of people in one organization will set out to manipulate and modify the behaviour of people in another place within or beyond their own perceived boundary. We often hear the expressions 'deliver the curriculum' or 'drive through changes', and these expressions reflect this belief that we must have an effect on others through our directed activity. Yet quantum physics tells us that there is no distance between objects and that the whole idea of single or separate objects has no basis in reality. We learn from quantum physics that common-sense ideas of causality are not the only ways of connecting things together, and yet, faced with this observation, we respond with disbelief or a feeling of inadequacy as to how to respond.

'Either/or' ways of thinking are drawn into question by quantum physics, where it is suggested that we have to learn to develop the adaptive principles of 'both/and' thinking. For example: we can think of the whole school, and we can think of the individuals; we fix our attention on one or the other, but in reality they exist and continue to operate at the same time, and whatever happens as we attend to one aspect of them will have other consequences and effects elsewhere. This inherent uncertainty, the both/and character of the school/learner, replaces our usual fixation on one aspect and demands that we begin to try and extend our ways of seeing to accommodate a more beneficial view, more akin to the growing understanding of the dynamic reality of the world and more aligned to the ways in which we are beginning to understand how our brains manage to learn (Wilson, 1999).

In short, we have to learn to see improvement in more contextualized ways. Drawing upon this interpretive view of school inside a wider system, where both and each have to be recognized as influencing and influenced, we can begin to have conversations on change from multiple perspectives: not just as the schools were, as a result of the last inspection, but as they are today as a result of observations from staff, students, parents, governors, where they might be going, and what they will possibly become. The insights lead us towards a more sustainable, participatory and inclusive debate that examines school purpose, values, and the learning and teaching process and how to connect and work usefully within a wider community of schools.

In the next chapter I will explore the type of methodology which will allow us to see how the reconceptualization of improvement moves our discussion away from instrumental strategy to a different form of approach, which attempts to establish school and intra-school networks where growth becomes mutually supportive. This is reform that liberates and provides a sustainable method for schools to learn with and from.

KEY ISSUES AND IDEAS IN THIS CHAPTER:

- I have suggested that schools are told to change in particular ways, and that in doing this they become dependent on operating within the approved approaches, where deviation implies weakness. This improvement process would be tolerable if the conditions within which schools were changing were controllable and manageable at the same pace. They are not. Consequently the ideas that are driving improvement are in decline in the wider world and yet maintain kudos within the school system.
- The result is that any innovative design is viewed by schools as suspicious and challenging, because schools themselves are under the watchful eye of external agencies whose role it is to maintain rather then innovate.
- The necessity to disturb the balance between maintenance and development couldn't be greater in all parts of the system, but disturbance is unlikely to happen because if schools do move too far into disequilibrium they run the risk of being charged with negligence and inappropriate behaviour.
- I suggest that we are now reaching a crisis point in schooling which I believe will lead to radical shifts attempting to introduce new forms of learning into a newly conceptualized system. This system will include schools, but in a designed manner that is different from that which we have experienced across the past 100 years.
- The alternative approaches demand a different way of seeing school improvement and a different way of doing school improvement. They associate

different metaphors and meaning to the organization that we describe as the school. The metaphors that we choose to describe our schools are politically, socially and historically driven and they are now in contested territory. Some rise up as new definitions of an emerging organizational learning, while other metaphors will fade as they decline from their once dominant and influential position of value in society. If a culture determines that the school system is to be developed and monitored solely through mechanistic methods, then the resulting perceptions of learning and of education will be inhibited by that model and restricted to those few areas in which it can exercise a sense of control and into which it can establish management practices. This is the reality of the present, based on the world view of the past, but it will not work in the longer term, and schools will be disgraced as a result because they will not be able to succeed, despite their best efforts to do so. This will happen not because any one person engineers it that way, but because the prevailing powers and values of the past will influence and mess up the best laid plans.

- I have argued that our ways of thinking on this matter are at a transformational point. I suggest that the early part of the next century will be the watershed, in which we move away from the modernistic ways in which control and order were paramount, into a new systemic view in which previously established boundaries break or are broken down. This will be driven by learning that is sustained at the political, economic, environmental, social and technical levels on the local and global stage.

NOTE

1 This chapter is a modified version of a paper first presented at ICSEI (International Congress for School Effectiveness and Improvement) 1998 by P. Clarke, J. Reed and C. Lodge.

Chapter 4

Finding the Path

> *The market system has become phenomenally sophisticated at managing what could be called first-order exchanges – like buying a car, a loaf of bread or a television set, in which it is unnecessary to have any continuing relationship with the partner to exchange. But it is less sophisticated at second-order exchanges which, like most human relationships, depend upon reciprocal understandings*
> Geoff Mulgan, *Connexity*

In this chapter I want to provide a route map which systemically conceptualizes school improvement. This will allow users to locate the improvement work within a contextual frame of reference through which strategic improvement intentions can be made more transparent. At the start of the book, I asked two questions which underpin the nature of the search I am undertaking in this book. By way of reminder I revisit them here:

- How is the 'search' for wholeness to be *expressed* within our schools so that staff and students might make a personal and a collective sense of what it is that they are moving into and participating in, rather than being bystanders in someone else's plan, made insignificant and voiceless by the sheer immensity of the system?
- How is the 'search' for a sense of wholeness to be *achieved* in a school system which has built itself on the maintenance of artificial boundaries and subject specialisms, where the environments in which we establish and focus what we call learning are controlled by linear structures and where the specialisms serve to fragment, disassemble and inhibit the construction of integrated meaning?

I suggested that two important themes emerge in these questions. They concern the 'expression' of the school system – 'How might we begin to describe the types of thinking, structure, ways of living and working, and a way of seeing the school in this mindset?' – and the 'achievement' of the school system – 'What might we do to get there?' These questions are both concerned with the process of improvement. They are conceptually important questions for us to consider and respond to, if we are to make headway from an instrumental to a sustainable system.

For a long time I have grappled with this part of the search. It is difficult territory. I have tried out the ideas with teachers and senior LEA staff involved directly in trying to influence change, I have talked with parents about the long-term desires they have for their children, and I have listened to eminent speakers at many conferences who are all in their own ways trying to make some sense out of this puzzle.

The material that I present here is my current best attempt to make sense of these ideas and experiences about transition from one way of living, thinking and seeing change to another, in a way that captures the essential components that will explain systemically the contexts of two paradigms, the modern and the eco-logical, and which will illuminate the transitional ground between these two perspectives being touched upon at this time.

I am concerned that the chapter might be misinterpreted as a methodology of improvement. I can see why this might be the case, and I want to suggest here that if you intend to use it as such, think hard about what approach to its use you are taking. If your developmental view is driven from the instrumental, modern paradigm, you might try to change what your organization does in order to establish some of the concepts in the transitional or the ecological paradigm. Your approach to achieving these integrative concepts would remain embedded inside the old design of how to think, and I believe you would remain frustrated. If you are to engage with the concepts from a perspective aligned to an ecological paradigm, I think you have to come to terms with the matter of transcendence (Knudsen, 1999) a process which is at work when we raise questions and place possible futures in front of people and which takes us beyond the instrumental and encourages us to let go of inhibited control of the immediate context and accept that the naturally intuitive, synthesizing, inquiring human mind will make sense of what is happening and will in time see the transition. As I said at the start of the book, this is a matter of consciousness. We can facilitate the shift by developing co-operative, quality-oriented, partnership-based inquiry that seeks sustainable practice whilst remaining adaptive to new demands, and we can design networks, but we cannot mandate a change of ways of seeing. That is a question of influence, of value, of creating something more akin to what the human spirit feels is going to be a better way of doing things, and that will be a paradigmatic shift. So, asking how we might express the thinking prompts an investigation into concepts and stimulates the possibility of other ways of doing schools. Asking how to achieve the expression inside the present paradigm automatically assumes action of some kind. Systemic thinking challenges this assumption and draws our attention to preparing the contexts, the networks and the partnerships within which we will begin to see the problems we face in a different way.

THINKING IMPROVEMENT

So far in this book, I have tried to outline some of the emerging argument which can provide some structure and location for the various kinds of 'improvement' activity undertaken in schools or upon schools by others. I have argued that many of the efforts to improve the present school system are modelled on a modern conceptualization of schooling that seeks to minimize learner and organizational failure rather than maximize the possibilities of success. These approaches take an unconsciously deterministic view of events, seeing unpredictability as a weak-ness and therefore constraining possible outcomes and freedoms. This approach has evolved out of designs modelled around the needs of the industrial age to create the next generation of workers, and, as such, schools engage in a series of 'first-order' (Mulgan, 1998) learning transactions with students which have commodified learning into discrete packages of subjects, lacking interrelatedness and coherence.

As the information age has emerged rapidly in recent years, it has brought with it demands for a different way of understanding learning that can adapt within an unpredictable environment. On both a personal and an organizational level, there has been a change. This change has taken us from a life that was largely organized by the state or by the company, once it was opted into, to a world where everyone is in charge of their own destiny (Handy, 1998). This observation is starkly evident in a recent British government study (1996) and illustrates the fact that most of our lives, after we leave school, are only loosely connected to work institutions.

Table 4.1 *Percentage of labour force in different types of employment (%)*

Type of employment	1985	1995	2005
Part-time	21	24	25
Self-employed	11	13	13.5
Temporary	5	6	8
Permanent	84	82	79

Source: *Labour market flexibility: Business strategies*, London (cited in Handy, 1998, p. 70).

If an 8 per cent (1995 figure) unemployment rate is added to the combined total of part-time, self-employed and temporary workers, we reach 51 per cent in 1995 outside the full-time employment scene. Handy (1998) suggests that this is 'the visible sign of a new flexibility', as it is matched within full-time employment, where the 'average' span of a permanent job is now six years and a permanent career is perhaps better seen as a succession of six-year jobs and is thus itself a flexible rather than a static phenomenon. In such an environment, adaptivity to the experience of uncertainty is a necessary skill.

This skill takes the form of interactions that can formulate what Kegan (1994) calls 'systemic knowing' – an appreciation by those who work inside an organizational culture of the underlying structures that facilitate ways of thinking, living, working and seeing the relationship between organization, people and environment (Csikszentmihalyi, 1990, 1993, 1997). Systemic knowing is achieved through collaboration with colleagues; it develops as they collectively establish group identity and group norms. In learning schools this can be achieved through identification, practice and refinement of what individual teachers and their colleagues are good at and what they need to develop further, which is then shared across a wider network to ensure system-wide recognition of a new, beneficial influencing factor.

Correspondingly, school improvement has to evolve from being interpreted as dealing with structural change promoting desired attributes such as plans, policies and management mechanisms. Whilst these attributes are geared towards optimizing learner output in examinations in the form of first-order exchanges, they do this at the expense of second-order changes to underlying organizational culture, which offer the longer-term strategic means of survival, self-expression and sustainability. I have suggested that where the past activities of the effectiveness and improvement community symbolize the final 'dance of the fossils' (Baudrillard, 1994), they might also express the 'end of the beginning', having moved schools from modern towards beyond-modern or intermediate means of working. Their legacy is to have heightened professional awareness of accountability to all learners, and to ensure that the systems designed are of the very highest quality.

However, as attention turns towards learning and learning systems (Schein, 1992) and how best to support learning at personal and organizational levels, there is a corresponding demand for different types of improvement approach to those that have come before. In short, there is a need for a reconceptualization of the improvement 'problem' so that it can take us into the improvement of learning and ensure adaptive, emergent and sustainable practices.

Schools seem to lack a conceptual language (Morgan, 1986) with which to describe the change process that is being experienced and that can be shared and collectively explored for this learning agenda to flourish. The modelling language would be useful because it could assist staff to share and to clarify their insights and use them as the foundation for further knowledge-generating activity with both relevance and value to their personal and organizational lives.

I want to pause here for a moment and turn to my first question: How is the 'search' for wholeness to be expressed within our schools so that staff and students might make a personal and a collective sense of what it is that they are moving into and participating in? I want to try to capture these ideas in a form that graphically compares where I believe we have come from, to where I think we are headed in the improvement of our schools as we begin to refocus on learning. To do this I want to use the term 'configuration' as a container (Miles and Huberman, 1994) for the characteristics that might be used to describe the concepts of the school. If schools represent different configurations of organizational cultures (Hargreaves, 1995), each being a variation on a similar theme, then the configuration of each of these cultures can be said to be 'constituted' differently. In order to enhance our conceptual view of school improvement so that it better suits the present and immediate future, I think we need to begin to look at these differing 'constitutional configurations' holistically rather than breaking the activity of the school down into separate, isolated concepts. We need to systematize our conceptual view.

To achieve this we can ask ourselves some 'generative' questions – ones that will move along with what we find and stimulate further investigation about what we observe when we look at a school engaged in improvement work and consider what the sum of the different types of activity represented in the school improvement activity represents, in terms of how the organization might be 'thinking', how it lives out these activities and uses them to inform its work, and how it establishes and maintains extended relationships that it sees as being valuable and worth pursuing. In seeking evidence to illustrate and inform each of these generative questions we will be able to look at the methods the school uses to improve, and these will illustrate the type of organizational structure which it takes for granted as a natural way of working. Different schools will illustrate each of these configuration points differently, through their practice and through their selection of particular types of improvement intervention. In my quest to make greater sense of school improvement, I recognize three phases of school growth, described in Table 4.2.

In earlier pages of this book, I have challenged the school formulation based on the modern paradigm as outlined above, suggesting that it suits a bygone era despite its prevalence in the contemporary setting. I challenge the individualistic orientation of schooling, arguing that is serves no long-term societal benefit; I suggest instead that both individual and social features of learning must now have status within the new concept of the school.

DISTANT VOICES HEARD FOR THE FIRST TIME

This reconceptualization places a pedagogic demand on how to 'teach' students to work together. School improvement has in the past emphasized this at the interpersonal level, to facilitate the managerial effectiveness of whole-school/corporate approaches, but has frequently failed to emphasize the necessity of strategies which can at the same time develop a cognitive and intra-personal change from modern to beyond-modern approaches.

If we take such an agenda seriously, and want to establish learning schools, the engagement of the learner inside the choice-making process of the learning content and learning process must be recognized and worked on. As Jackson *et al.* (1998) recently suggested, the concept of students as researchers challenges both of the present system and teacher expectations of how that system should function. I would add that it challenges the status quo because it taps into and redefines the cognitive and intrapersonal mindset – it challenges ways of thinking and ways of seeing school. Jackson and colleagues (*ibid.*) proceed to make a useful distinction between student learning and joint learning, arguing that the themes of learning engage staff and students in 'joint learning', with which they are able to develop their learning community further.

Examples such as these, and others that I will develop in Chapters 5 and 6, are beginning to provide evidence of the emergence of a 'beyond-modern transition' taking place in school (Table 4.2). What we witness as the contested territory of the cognitive, interpersonal and intrapersonal debates concerning how best to run schools within each paradigm will inevitably shift as more and more schools begin to redesign the learning/student/teacher relationship. The modern paradigm, beyond-modern transitions and ecological paradigms (Table 4.2) will each have a position on this matter, and the contested territory arises when these positions rub up against each other. They may be transitory within school cultures but remain contested in the wider societal debate, because such ideas take considerably longer to embed and establish themselves in the mainstream. Therefore we witness schools that might display examples of a good deal of beyond-modern practice but will be continually pulled back into the dominant modern paradigm until there is a major contextual shift.

However, in saying this, I believe that this direction is set and that we are going to move in the coming century increasingly towards the beyond-modern,

Table 4.2 *A map of phases of school growth*

	Ways of thinking (cognitive)	Ways of living and working (Inter-personal)	Ways of seeing (Intra-personal)	Seeking	Assumed underlying structure
Modern paradigm	Generalizes Hypothesizes Proposes Assumes cause and effect Ideals and values	Hierarchical Role-conscious	Subjective	Concrete – certainty in outcomes Accepting of points of view – but not changing own position	Individualistic: Single categories: self/class/ dept–dept/ key stage– key stage/ school
Beyond-modern transitions	Abstract systems – ideology formulating Establishing relations between abstractions	Institution Relationship-regulating forms Conscious of multiple role	Self-development Self-regulation Self-formation Identity	Abstractions less than certain, increasing willingness for flexibility Mutual needs recognized Interpersonal activity attended to	Integrative: networked Complex systems: self/dept-dept/key stage–key stage/school to school
Ecological paradigm	Dialectical Testing formulation Paradox, contradiction Oppositeness Complexity	Inter-institutional Relationship between forms Recognized inter-connections between self and others	Inter-connection of self and others Inter-individualiza-tion – a 'part' of, and 'apart' from	Abstract systems Ideological Flexible and adaptive – contested Institutional relationships Self-development Self-regulation	Communities: Complex networked system:dept-dept/key stage–key stage/ school-school/ school within other networked systems

transitional school, which will in turn open up further the arguments for and understanding of an ecological conceptualization of learning and the institution of the school, characteristics of which I have outlined in Chapter 2 and revisit here.

In describing school improvement in this way, and linking it to some emerging themes of learning and thinking about learning, we begin to identify sustainable themes in the conceptualization of improvement, where

- the future is not some place we are going, but emerges as we influence and are influenced by what we do, how we think and learn;
- many of these paths are not found but made;
- the making of these pathways changes both the maker and the destination. (Khan, 1996)

School improvement already challenges the past orthodoxy and has moved schools towards the beyond-modern transitions of interpersonal activity that are concerned with transparent regulation and operation within a complex system, with emphasis on regulation of self and accountability through institution. However, it has undertaken this without necessarily paying attention to how strategic activity might also have to change people's ways of thinking, enabling them to think with a different, 'beyond-modern transitional' outlook. Many staff remain completely detached from a sense of real engagement because they have had to

Table 4.3 *Student learning and joint learning*

Student learning	Joint learning
Academic learning: interpreting data, understanding complex issues, skills of investigation	Using the learning attributes identified to help to **See different issues** and to **See issues differently**
Individual learning: self-knowledge, confidence	
Interpersonal learning: listening skills, understanding others	
Civic learning: understanding rights and responsibilities, working on behalf of others	
Communal learning: caring for and about each other, understanding what it is really like to be at school, helping school to be a better place	
Disappointment and regret: things that you feel negative about or wish had been different	

Source: Jackson *et al.* (1998).

implement an agenda without redefining their voice, and therefore have opted out and reinforce an intrapersonally bound and modern way of living and working because they have no opportunity in which to have a 'change-conversation'.

As a result we witness the tensions between ideas in ascendency and decline suggested in Chapter 3. They are tensions between paradigms, and between individual and organizational growth trajectories (Gray *et al.*, 1999, Cuttance, 1994). On an interpersonal and intrapersonal level it may be possible to undertake a 'beyond-modern' perspective, but if the organizational way of thinking is in its

Table 4.4 *Ecological conceptualization of learning*

Learning	Thinking about learning
People have access to learning 24 hours a day, 365 days a year, through a variety of sources, some of which will be schools	People can learn things from many sources
Teachers are employed to match teaching to the needs of the learner	Everyone must understand the learning process and have basic learning skills
Schools are learning communities where everyone (students, teachers, parents, administrators) is both a learner and a teacher, depending on the circumstances	The learning process is controlled by the learner. What is to be taught, when it should be taught and how it should be taught will all be determined by the learner
Information is accessed according to the learner's capability and interest. The information will vary greatly after basic skills are learned	Education and learning are highly interactive activities. Success is based on how well learners work together as a team
Schools as we know them have been dramatically altered in form and function, or have been replaced	Formal education is the basis for lifelong learning
Communities will be responsible for the education of both students and adults. Business and industry will be actively involved in school developments	'School' is only one of a multitude of steps in the education journey
Formal education institutions are subject to 'market' forces	The more capability and adaptability you have the more successful you will be
	Basic education is funded by both government and is supported by community and private sources

modern description demonstrating its 'thinking' through abstractions, there will inevitably be a clash of perspectives and organizational turbulence.

Finally, if we look at the ecological paradigm we can witness the ascending ideas of integrated contextual thinking. We can already witness these ideas in practice through some examples of intra-school networks. But we can also anticipate that we will not achieve the transcendent systemic benefits at this time because we will have numerous schools and individuals in those schools working at earlier stages of the matrix, in modern and beyond-modern cognitive, inter-personal and intrapersonal mindsets.

What I have briefly described is a conceptual map with which to move into the new territory of improvement and begin to assist strategic thinking about the activity taking place in each of the paradigms and in the transitional domain, in order to comprehend better what schools are doing and to improve our under-standing of intervention. I appreciate that this is difficult material. As I said at the beginning of the book, this approach to improvement is explicitly value-driven and comes to you as a reader inside an educational paradigm which at present claims the benefits of being value-free. I have also suggested that the material is presented here in the form of a search and that part of that search is for a language with which to describe the complexity of our journey into systemic understanding. I think this map does help with providing a broader view of *what* is happening *where* as improvements embed, and *what* is likely to be inhibiting change from happening, and I have found this when I have used it with colleagues involved in strategic planning. It is through reference to this conceptual map that we have begun to develop a more constructive language of change.

LIVING AND WORKING IMPROVEMENT: THE LEARNING JOURNEY AS A PROCESS OF EMERGENT UNDERSTANDING

I now turn to my second question: How is the 'search' for a sense of wholeness to be *achieved* in a school system?

To do this I believe that we need to redesign our modelling language so that we begin to consider each school 'configuration' as a unique constitutional configuration, and we then place that within a wider context through which we are able to make greater sense of why and how the school functions as it does within its localized setting.

1 The importance of difference: different journeys on a similar map

The concepts of the modern paradigm, beyond-modern transitions, and ecological paradigm amplify the observation that schools are uniquely configured. However, it appears to me that whilst the schools I work in are generally moving into similar territory of transition from modern to beyond-modern forms of organizational and cognitive, interpersonal and intrapersonal activity, sharing the same map as it were, their improvement journeys are quite different. Given that this is happening, what might be done to support schools as they attempt to achieve the change and to realize its emancipatory ambition? I have used a series of simple approaches to do this. To capture the differences it is necessary to work closely with staff and to share with them observations, ideas and data-gathering instruments.

Sustained conversation is key. Talk can be emancipatory. My work with schools always seeks to be designed as longitudinal study, where the critical issue concerns taking the time to hear what is happening on the ground. If it is an expected part of the organizational culture of a learning school to be creative, to engage in risk-taking, and to be innovative and open to new ideas, then the methods used to facilitate this way of working have to support and encourage a climate of care and trust. Freire (1973) described the attitudes which fostered a 'true dialogue' as those which underpin democratic, empowering leadership and societal change. These attitudes are those which nurture responsive and creative thinking because they develop a climate within which risk can occur without penalty. They are:

1. Love: 'Dialogue . . . cannot exist in the absence of a profound love for the world and for human beings.'
2. Humility: 'Dialogue . . . is broken if the parties lack humility. How can I dialogue if I always project ignorance on others and never perceive my own?'
3. Faith: 'Dialogue . . . requires an intense faith in people, faith in their power to make and re-make, to create and re-create, faith in their vocation to be more fully human.'
4. Trust: 'Dialogue becomes a horizontal relationship of which mutual trust between the participants is the logical consequence.'
5. Hope: 'Dialogue cannot be carried on in a climate of hopelessness. If the participants expect nothing to come of their effort, their encounter will be empty, sterile, bureaucratic, and tedious.'
6. Critical thinking: 'True dialogue cannot exist unless the participants engage in critical thinking. The important thing is the continuing transformation of reality on behalf of the continuing humanization of people.'
   (Freire, 1973, pp. 78–81)

A sustained conversation with a school designed around these themes makes the value of human interaction a core concern.

2 School as a learning place: knowledge generation

The last decade or so has seen considerable change. Activity in school is being focused primarily on modernizing the interpersonal ways of working within the institution. This has prepared schools to recognize that change is a feature of their organizational lives and that it is a necessary way of thinking if they are to operate successfully within a complex system. However, this recognition does not necessarily result in schools and teachers using change activity to realign and redefine their cognitive approach (ways of thinking) constructively so as to complement the beyond-modern transitional school. In fact I would suggest that schools remain for the most part locked inside an intrapersonal way of seeing which services immediate needs and accepts points of view at the interpersonal level in very modern ways. So, whilst they are change 'aware', formulating plans, and developing complex system-wide intentions, they are not necessarily change 'smart', as they are missing important features of an improvement repertoire that will facilitate their desired agenda.

Observing that schools might change, but might not use 'change knowledge' drawn from changing, has caused me to ask how to begin to challenge teachers' thinking about change so that their school-created 'change knowledge' can be put to much better use. What might be done to develop approaches that encourage inter-school connections, where teachers have an opportunity to observe, listen to, and use strategies and techniques that will extend their personal repertoire and at the same time enhance their systemic understanding?

In a series of projects I have worked with colleagues to design new systems that will amplify areas of 'similarity' and areas of 'difference' in teaching and learning. Improvement work should stress 'difference' rather than 'similarity' as it has a trajectory towards the developmental rather than the maintenance agenda. An appreciation of the distinction between closed and open-ended change (see Chapter 2, Table 2.4) facilitates this importance of difference; closed change focuses on maintaining what we have already established.

Getting teachers to consider similarity (patterns of similar activity) and difference in their teaching and learning requires teachers to explore each other's teaching styles and to challenge them critically as well as inviting alternatives. Once a staff arrives at the recognition of difference they begin to have strategic conversations about the implications of such difference, because the process generates questions. For example, does it matter if one teacher teaches a class in one way, and another teacher works with the same class using a different approach? What messages do our different ways of teaching give to students? How can we find out what the students think about each teacher's approach? What would we do if we found that the responses we gathered indicated that we had to change our ways of working? Are we willing to pursue this agenda and live with the consequences?

Here I am drawn back to Michael Fullan's (1991) observation that 'change is a process and not an event'. This matters. It matters because it provides us with a gateway to conceptualizing the improvement activity of a learning school as an unfolding of the 'reciprocal understandings' to which Mulgan (1998) refers at the start of this chapter. These 'understandings' are worked on by all members of a learning school community, in differing degrees of intensity and awareness according to how important the matter is to their school, key stage, class, student/group or personal agendas and how 'change aware'[1] they might be.

The process of constructing understanding – of generating knowledge about our teaching and learning – is inevitably messy and unpredictable, for it crosses boundaries between what teachers feel confident about and what they do not. It unfolds in ways that we might not expect because it is dealing with the development of new learning inside a living system, where different people are interpreting at different points within these boundaries. As this new learning evolves and becomes embedded, changes will happen in the workplace that illustrate the profound significance of Fullan's message. Teachers begin to talk differently about what they are teaching, learning resources are developed that are more suited to the learners' needs and interests, the dynamics of the staff meetings shift from technical administrative minutiae to a focus on learning. Fullan is asking us to rethink how we undertake change, asking us to 'see' improvement differently. It is this looking out for the small, unobtrusive but significant indicators and being able to talk about them and share their salience that is a part of this awakening awareness, a part of the rethinking.

3 Multi-site learning: the integrated network

This led me in my work to a second feature of reconceptualizing the improvement agenda: I was concerned that, if an approach were to be developed, it could be applied to all schools, because the 'knowledge generation' concept ought to imply more than single-site operation, otherwise it would remain individually locked inside the modern paradigm, where the danger of 'groupthink' (Hargreaves, 1994) holds the school within a view of organizational reality that is self-repeating. It would need to assume a structure that reflected some of the ideas of a complex learning system, and this would necessitate a multiplicity of perspectives on the same issue, demanding more than single-site perspectives, more than teachers' viewpoints of learning within the present paradigm.

It was necessary, therefore, to develop principles which would underpin a learning process that could be shared, articulated and understood by schools in their daily experience of improvement, no matter where they might be located on the orders of growth 'map', and that facilitated the need for a network of schools. I have worked in a number of these, in particular in Bury and Tameside LEAs. The general guiding principles of operation on which these networks have been based are these:

- **The learning process is about maintaining a focus on what matters.** This concerns learning itself, and how teaching is enabling that learning to occur. It also relates to the environment within which that learning is taking place. We can ask: is the focus conducive to learning and does it reflect what people believe in and are committed to improve?
- **The learning process is about sustaining conversation and interaction** (Huberman 1993). This focus is on the importance of a shared and sustained conversation amongst all stakeholders in the school. It pays attention to what is happening as the school evolves. This conversation happens in two ways,
  - the level of event – what we might be doing,
  - the level of process – what are we learning from doing this?

The first of these principles gives considerable information on what the school or teacher needs to attend to and how they might be doing this; the second gives us information on why they are doing it in the way they are. Conversation of this type captures a key question – 'What matters to us here?' – and allows people to illuminate and amplify core areas of concern, raising awareness of the underlying structure of a complex system.

- **The learning process is about living with the complexity of incomplete-ness.** This focus is on an acceptance of the partial, emerging picture, rather than the completed view. We live and work with partial data, and our efforts in pursuing improved learning are to promote activity that leads to a greater understanding and clarity. It captures the question: 'What might we usefully want to learn more about that can develop our intra-institutional learning?'
- **The learning process is one of application and observation.** This focus is on use: it explores with all stakeholders the opportunity to bring forth different ways of explaining, legitimizing and celebrating success and weakness. It captures the key question: 'How are we using our learning?'
- **The learning process is one of theory generation.** This focus is on the need to be knowledge generators in school, between schools and inside a local community – formulating and redesigning ideas. Stakeholders create new understanding about learning and teaching which informs others in the com-munity of what works. This new knowledge might then attract or draw upon knowledge created from beyond the school. It captures a key question: 'How are we making sense of what we are learning and using this to develop relationships that are sustainable and mutually beneficial?'

To begin to make sense of these concepts we have to accept that there will be a series of ongoing, overlapping experiences that at times will combine and provide clarity, but which at other times will be muddled and fuzzy (Kosko, 1993). These lie at the interface of points on the growth map.

These ideas have emerged as a result of trying to 'live' through change and 'work' out the contradictions and paradoxes that we have faced as we have developed our understanding of how to work within and between schools in the pursuit of improved performance, I will describe one such network in greater detail in Part 2. The final component of the approach that I want to describe here concerns how to 'see' the improvement problem.

4 Seeing improvement as a living learning system

Advocates of living systems thinking (see Capra, 1996) argue that earlier forms of describing systems (Senge, 1990) fail to see the world as it really is, as a constantly pulsating, changing, complex weave of interconnected and interacting relation-ships through which order naturally emerges from chaos (Capra, 1996). Living systems thinking has emerged from the world of new sciences. It draws inspira-tion and insights from the natural world seen through the eyes of quantum physics, ecology, complexity and chaos theory.

Theorists of living systems argue that, just as in the natural world, human groupings are self-organizing and emergent and the flow of information through an organization takes its own course. If people are connected and meet in a con-ducive organizational environment, the resulting interactions will be beneficial and will reframe their activity in purposeful ways. Instead of seeking specific points at which to intervene and target, living systems thinkers suggest that it is more productive personally and organizationally to develop the ability of the people working in the organization to recognize the direction in which the system is moving and, through intensifying their awareness of this, to be aware of new behaviour which it has prompted and which moves the system into new forms of activity, new trajectories of interest (Bohm, 1992). The map of phases of school growth I outlined earlier in this chapter (see Table 4.2) provides some idea of where these new journeys might take schools within a modern paradigm, a beyond-modern transitional phase and an ecological paradigm.

If improvement is to work, it seems to me that it has to be authentic and profoundly personal to the individuals and the organization; they have to own what one headteacher recently told me was their 'mantra of change'. This arises out of 'a personal and imaginative creativity that transcends analysis' (Badaracco and Ellsworth, 1989). It is developed through the creative fusion of ideas inside a community of learners. This is likely, under present constraints, to be an intensely localized experience. If learning schools are to transcend their present boundaries, if they are to move from modern to beyond-modern and to an ecological paradigm, then teachers need to be able both to see their system, to understand and use structures to promote new ideas successfully, and to talk about these ideas on learning to others.

> *Here is a tree.*
> *It is also a system.*
> *It is a system that connects the ground to the sky.*
> *(Alice, aged 11)*

Seeing this living system in action is a daily event. It is evident in many of the routine activities of teachers such as the planning process, as they develop materials with learners. From the outset, the stage of listening to learners talking about their prior knowledge of a theme, to the excitement of setting a learning contract in motion with them, to the responses as suggestions and ideas get shared around the team in gathering material to suit the demands of the contract, there is an energy which is both powerful and contagious. Conveying to others the experience, the feelings, the reasons why the process is working, in such a way as to capture the essence of it and enthuse those colleagues who were not a part of the initial experience is much harder to do, but I believe we have to grasp this challenge and see if we can develop ways of meeting it.

To do this I have encouraged schools to keep a journal of their improvement activity and to share it in team meetings as a stimulus for recall of what has happened over the intervening weeks of meetings, and as a means of review over time. As schools begin to chart an organizational journey, as they initiate simple review procedures, they also initiate a search for greater clarity and meaning in their work by identifying patterns of activity, rituals, common experiences, areas of consistency and areas of difference, points where they intervene, points where they manage and points where they lead. What is interesting is that their observations seldom return to the meetings in the form of simple lists of events. They become enriched with small, seemingly insignificant contextualizing asides which add richness and emotion to the journeys they are taking. In the ISIS initiative, which I will report in more detail in the next chapter, we frequently found that the network meeting's only agenda item was reporting back and discussion, as staff from different schools became engrossed in each school's story of change and development. What I find fascinating is the detail of this process and how it relies heavily on processes of intuition and of teachers trying to put ideas into a deeper context rather than accepting the surface-level rationale. The process of encouraging a 'storying' of improvement initiates an holistic 'point of view' approach to change rather than beginning change from positions of order and intellectual analysis.

In his work on strategic planning, Mintzberg observes the same process happening: he suggests that it is the 'qualitative, rather than the quantitative' that captures the heart of an improvement agenda (Mintzberg, 1989). In a modern paradigm the search for concrete, certain strategy denies the possibility that a beyond-modern transitional and ecological paradigm can open up greater willingness to accept flexible and even contested starting points as the basis of improvement agendas. Both the modern and the ecological paradigms may be extremely sophisticated in their use and manipulation of data, but they are distinguished by the manner in which they meet needs, identify areas of concern, construct a new consensus for change, and listen to the 'secret harmonies' (Nias, 1989) of the school that draw on personal and collective judgement, interest and strengths, generating an authentic and committed belief in spending time on new ventures and distancing them from the previous ways of working. Fusing together a range of data sets and a range of voices (Clarke and Christie, 1996) means spending time investigating where the teachers need support in teaching and learning, fusing external agendas to internal needs and legitimizing the local over the broader demands coming from elsewhere. Ultimately it implies an organizational self-confidence, trust and instinctive feel for what it is right to do, and an ability to draw upon strategies that can service this approach. As Evans (1996, p. 201) suggests,

> To misunderstand this personal source of vision is to misunderstand
> the origins of strategy. When, as it all too often does, strategic
> planning begins by identifying external goals and then moves on to
> analysing internal strengths, it puts the cart before the horse.

Therefore, to capture this core mission and to understand truly how it will relate to its environment, a school must first understand *its own strengths* (Schein, 1985). It must ask itself, 'What are we good at here?' The next part of the book probes into this line of inquiry, through an analysis of a network and a schools case study.

KEY ISSUES AND IDEAS IN THIS CHAPTER

In this chapter I have suggested that:

- There is a need to get beyond simple instrumental approaches to improvement and to redesign the map of improvement to suit the demands of the information age.

- To do this I have proposed a conceptual framework which serves as a planning device for systemic development. It described ways of thinking (cognitive), living and working (interpersonal) and ways of seeing (intrapersonal) the reality of the world we seek to influence, characterized by modern, beyond modern and ecological paradigms.
- I suggest that this framework can provide a scaffold in the form of constitutional configurations with which to reflect critically upon a school improvement activity. These configurations present considerable challenges, some of which I indicated in Chapter 3, concerning power, self-organization in teams, multiplicities rather than single growth possibilities, a need to establish and promote a risk-taking culture, a need for time and, finally, a need for sustained discourse on the impact of the changes.
- I have indicated, and will revisit this in the second part of the book, how the map illuminates the reasons why we find change blocked in school, raising the importance of difference and differentiated intervention approaches in the improvement method.
- To facilitate understanding of the differential intervention which constitutional configurations indicate, I have suggested that we might usefully reflect on differing layers of the school as it now exists and be prepared to modify and evolve the layers of observation as and when it becomes necessary, rather than predetermine a strategy for development.
- I have suggested that a central concern in the reconceptualization of improvement is to ensure that schools become knowledge generators, as well as knowledge users, thus making them 'change smart' as they enhance their capacity for learning.
- I have revisited and emphasized the significance of Fullan's (1991) observation that change is a 'process and not an event' as an important way of seeing improvement and the 'reciprocal' understandings upon which successful improvement thrives.
- I have outlined a set of concepts which lie at the heart of what I believe is the learning process; these are concerned with focus, sustained conversation and interaction, incompleteness, application and observation, and theory generation.
- I have suggested that we might usefully wrap the improvement conceptualization within living systems thinking. This approach offers an holistic and authentic interpretation of how people and the systems they establish interrelate and flourish.

NOTE

1   By change aware I mean the extent to which both the individual teacher and the school think about change as having an effect on how they think, live and work in school, and the extent to which this thinking prompts them to see their activity differently.

Part 2: Living the Journey

In the first part of this book I established a basis for change centred around the distinction I have made between schooling and learning, suggesting that we were moving from modern ideas of schooling to an emergent systemic, ecological view, where the role and purpose of the school are radically redesigned to facilitate a shift of power and voice to the learner. Describing this, I argued that there is a necessary conceptual shift from one paradigm to the other, and that this shift is recognizable if we look at how schools go about the practice of school improvement, how they begin to describe their improvement activity in a different way, taking it from a series of events into a more purposeful and coherent process of renewal. I made a case for a method centred around knowledge generation, where learning schools become the reconstructors of their own reality and are actively involved in seeking out success and failure and paying attention to the process of improvement that has led to this, so that they can learn how they learn as organizations.

I believe that the resulting transitions from one way of working to another can be made explicit, and that we can both draw attention to the product of the debate on learning to improve – how we do it – and make explicit the technical language that assists us to frame our conceptual understanding of what we mean by the learning process. Paying attention to our discussions in this way forms a meta-language of improvement and serves as a means of establishing an organizational consciousness; it serves as a way of seeing schools from a new perspective, as participants in a bigger process of a learning system and as single units struggling to develop their own best routes.

In the planning of our journey I have argued that if we are to move towards seeing schools as learning communities we have to introduce a sustainable process to the practice of change, which will allow educators to focus primarily on improving their teaching in the service of better learning. I have suggested that this is best generated through educators engaging in collaborative activity. This activity is necessarily value-driven, it is integrative, and it recognizes that attempts to include and to encourage participation will result in practices that are better shared, better considered because of wider investigation, and better suited to localized demands. The integrative approach is undertaken with:

- an understanding of the importance of conversation sustained over time;
- an understanding of the importance of multiple perspectives in the search for meaning and deeper understanding;
- an awareness of the importance of incompleteness in our information and understanding – that our endeavour is to seek wholeness and unity of ideas but that this is a journey or search and is ongoing;

- an understanding that by experimentation with new possibilities for practice, and by ongoing assessment of the relationship between practice and the effects of practice, we can begin to redesign the 'learning map'.

These features constitute what I believe is a 're-norming' of school improvement, taking it from the modern, individualistic approach to one that begins to journey across a beyond-modern transitional ground of experiment and awareness-raising into systemic ecological thinking about schools inside integrated networks, operating collectively as evolving systems.

I think this is a long-term project. It will take two to three generations of sustained effort as learners come through and in turn take the conceptual and practical re-norming forward. It implies change at personal, institutional and interinstitutional levels, and for some time to come we will all be grappling with what it means to live with this complexity. The endgame is the creation of learning schools within learning communities, and these will be structurally supported by a transition from instrumental to sustainable practices which are sympathetic to a living system rather than a mechanical process of learning. This will happen through the naturally changing system, but it can be moved towards and accelerated through the exercise of conscious choice.

In this part of the book I will elaborate on these ideas by demonstrating how some LEAs and schools assist in, or inform and change, their teaching and learning activity and how this bears witness to the changing conceptualization of school. The material provides some of the landscape along an improvement journey.

In itself the material might not appear very different from what you might already be doing or have done; it is familiar terrain for many schools. But, as in any journey, different people, as they travel the same road, can observe different things and arrive with quite different interpretations of what they feel it was of value to see.

I will describe some of the journeys in the next two chapters. The descriptions represent different profiles of school activity, in the first example through a longitudinal initiative which was deliberately network-driven and in the second example through a school journey. I will show how in their own ways, they both illustrate the importance of difference as a strength in the development of the learning system, where this diversity of strategy offers all schools a vast resource base upon which they can draw and from which they can gain inspiration, ideas and approaches to improve their own work.

Chapter 5

Expeditions into Learning: N
on Establishing Knowledge-
Generating and
Knowledge-Using Systems

> *'The best thing for being sad,' replied Merlin, 'is to learn something.*
> *That is the only thing that never fails. You may grow old and*
> *trembling in your anatomies, you may lie awake at night listening*
> *to the disorder of your veins, you may see the world around you*
> *devastated by evil lunatics. There is only one thing for it then – to*
> *learn. Learn why the world wags and what wags it. That is the only*
> *thing which the mind can never exhaust, never alienate, never be*
> *tortured by, never fear or distrust, and never dream of regretting.*
> *Learning is the thing for you.'*
> T.H.White, *The Once and Future King*

Over the past five years I have been fortunate to have had the chance to work with schools and LEA staff in a number of projects, each of which has had as a core feature the intention of creating a more reflective, knowledge-generating culture inside the school community. The discussion in this chapter captures some of the main features of this work. I have chosen to focus primarily on one longitudinal initiative, but I draw from the experience of the other three projects in Bury, Cheshire and Wigan LEAs.

ISIS: JOURNEYS INTO SYSTEMIC LEARNING

The Improving Standards in Schools (ISIS) initiative has been operating in Tameside LEA, Greater Manchester, since 1995. From the outset, all the projects taking place within the ISIS initiative shared a common theme, aiming to develop systems which were locally sensitive and which could focus school attention on the improved performance of students. In that sense they were all integrative in their orientation, since they had as a common base of value the idea of co-operating for improvement, focusing on quality in teaching and learning, developing inter- and intra-school partnerships, and sharing successes where possible to establish sustainable improvement processes.

In each case there was an intra- and an inter-school dimension in the designs of the projects, where participants wanted to draw upon the school knowledge base and extend it through networks within the community of local schools. They did this in an attempt to enhance staff awareness of the diversity of approaches to improvement, to broaden their knowledge base of 'what works' and to encourage ıntra-school learning with colleagues. Furthermore, the intra-school dimension encouraged a critical climate for improvement, where differences could be examined, offered schools the chance to redesign and modify their work and provided all involved with a chance to look into the future and share insights and ideas about how to influence what might happen.

Table 5.1 *The conceptual orientation of the improvement projects*

	Ways of thinking (cognitive)	Ways of living and working (inter-personal)	Ways of seeing (intra-personal)	Seeking	Assumed underlying structure
Modern paradigm	Generalizes Hypothesizes Proposes Assumes cause and effect Ideals and values	Hierarchical Role-conscious	Subjective	Concrete – certainty in outcomes Accepting of points of view – but not changing own position	Individualistic: Single categories: self/class/ dept–dept/ key stage– key stage school
Beyond-modern transitions	Abstract systems – ideology formulating Establishing relations between abstractions	Institution Relationship-regulating forms Conscious of multiple role	Self-development Self-regulation Self-formation Identity	Abstractions less than certain, increasing willingness for flexibility Mutual needs recognized Interpersonal activity attended to	Integrative: networked Complex systems: Self/dept-dept/key stage – key stage/school to school

Our orientation for improvement was towards the 'beyond-modern transition', which would sow the seeds for a longer-term movement towards an integrated, networked ecological system. To give a flavour of the work of the initiatives I will describe some of the activity taking place in them, then I will draw together what I think are the significant themes that we have learnt during the development of these individual systems within schools and which have led to a broader intra-school networked system.

Founding principles

This system focused on the provision of longitudinal support sustained through the use of adviser, consultant and network teams. This support had a focus on school-based activity that sought to enhance student performance outcomes within the arena of legislative requirements:

> to support secondary schools in raising standards of achievement for students 11–16 in the context of national and LEA targets, by identifying and developing school strategies for the improvement of standards. (Smith *et al.*, 1996)

The ISIS initiative also sought to ensure that as well as improving standards it established a sustainable learning process. This promoted discussions, early in the development of the initiative, on the types of 'learning' principles that we should use to to guide the thinking behind our work. The ISIS team identified the following principles as being important to the philosophical approach of the initiative:

- The system we develop should be moving towards deeper and more complex reasons for learning;
- The system should see the development of data-rich and 'learning' strategies;
- The system should promote a context-specific and localized response to improvement, modelled on what staff believed mattered to them and their students;
- The system should include a broader definition of the meaning of 'success' in learning;
- The system should involve an investigation into learning and teaching processes that would enrich and enhance teacher and student performance.

Our aims were:

- to explore the range of methods and strategies used locally and nationally to tackle underachievement and raise standards;
- to set measurable and realistic targets for school improvement in the context of LEA and national targets;
- to plan and implement agreed strategies for improving standards;
- to develop effective and systematic ways of using school performance data to inform and support improvement;
- to evaluate the outcomes of improvement strategies;
- to create a culture for success within the school in order that improvements are sustained and embedded.

The design

The ISIS initiative was simple in design. Each year, a cohort of schools was invited to present a case to the LEA to become part of an inter-school network that would attract support from a consultant and LEA advisers. The schools presented a report that described their organizational goals, the approaches that they had taken in the past to school improvement and the challenges that they envisaged in the coming months as a result of their review of what was happening in school. They were asked to make some predictions of how their proposed approaches intended to impact on enhanced pupil performance and organizational practice.

Whilst this procedural hurdle allowed the LEA personnel to decide which schools should be a part of the initiative according to merit and necessity, it also served as a focusing device enabling the school staff to address the purposes behind their school improvement work. This inquiry also led schools to begin to investigate what was already successful in their own institutional setting and to initiate thinking on why it worked for them.

Once the schools were accepted within a cohort (there have been three to date, each involved in a two-year initial cycle), they were entitled to receive a package of additional support from the external sources of the LEA. This support included additional visits from the advisory team, seminar sessions and conferences with specialist speakers and the support of an external consultant. The school co-ordinator for the initiative was expected to attend cohort meetings off-site on behalf of the school and report half-termly to colleagues from other schools, and to advisers on their progress and on matters of concern. It was often these concerns that raised the most useful insights on the effects of the work in progress and served as a valuable indicators of the pressure schools and teachers face as their improvement initiatives coincide or conflict with externally demanded change.

Learning themes

Four important 'learning' themes underpinned the practice of the ISIS initiative:

Expanding minds

From the start of the initiative we felt that the involvement should always be seen as one of legitimized experiment. ISIS enabled schools to focus time and personnel resources on ideas that would perhaps otherwise remain aspects of their work which they would struggle to undertake, even though they often found that these were areas that, once initiated, seemed to have such significance that they wondered why they had put them off so long.

Making learning a priority

We were concerned that too much attention would be given to managerial activity in the improvement of standards in preference to learning. Having read and discussed the experiences of other improvement initiatives such as the Schools Make a Difference project (Myers, 1995), the IQEA (Improve the Quality of Education for All) work of Ainscow and colleagues (Ainscow *et al.*, 1994), from

Australia the work of Caldwell and Hayward (1998), Codding (1997) and Spring (1997), work from the USA (Smith, 1996; National Commission on Excellence in Education, 1983; Carnegie Corporation, 1983), and from Canada the Halton project in the Learning Consortium (Stoll and Fink, 1996), we wanted to take the lessons from these significant initiatives, but we wanted the schools to make sure that learning was their primary concern.

Establishing 'knowledge' as a shared commodity

We felt it was important to establish a culture of trust which would pursue in a collegial manner the issues that each school might raise and describe in the network meetings. The fundamental shared resource of the project was from the very start likely to be those ideas and approaches to improvement of teaching and learning that each school pursued for its own intentions. The structure of the ISIS project promoted the idea of a shared network, where co-ordinators from each of the schools could bring to the meetings updates of the projects they were involved in.

To begin with, we found there was an understandable concern about this approach. Schools in the network were geographically very close, in some cases fewer than five minutes' walk from each other. They were, and are, working in a context of neo-conservatism (Apple, 1998), where market values are expected to predominate in an educational arena. Our concerns related to the legacy of an ideology of individualism, and we were advocating the development of a learning community which would seek to develop integrated inter-school links for common benefit. Would teachers co-operate and share their insights and 'best practice' inside such a small network?

Mutual gains of networking

It became evident, however, that teachers were keen to share what they were doing with colleagues from other local schools. Their reasons were complicated but were based around interest in, and eagerness for, deeper insights into their own improvement activity. They told us that they felt happy to share their ideas because in so doing they gained by listening to other teachers' insights and suggestions, which could be applied to their own improvement work. In short, teachers in the network recognized that they could help themselves by helping others. An individualistic rationale was being serviced by integrative values! (This led me to reflect on the paradigm argument, and to realize that there was no reason why some schools would not take this approach and still evolve to the ecological paradigm.) The teachers wanted to know, at the simplest level, whether their experiences were unique; they wanted to know whether anyone had attempted 'their project' before, and, if so, what had they done and why had they done it in that way? They wanted to know about alternative insights that other schools had on the same issues. For example: in a teaching styles project, one school had developed a questionnaire. This was used in another school; the findings were shared and new themes were identified for each school to pursue. Teachers were fascinated by the difference in management and leadership of each other's schools. Some of the questions the meeting generated were recorded and shared with the teams:

- Why did the management take that approach?
- What did the rest of the staff think?
- How did the management respond to the dissent?
- Do they always do that?
- When the management introduced the agenda in its revised form, how did they change their approach?
- How do you make sure that staff have a say in this and aren't by-passed?

As the project developed and their trust increased, teachers wanted to know more about the approaches senior management were taking in each other's schools and whether these were assisting or inhibiting their opportunity to achieve commonly desired outcomes (see case study, Chapter 6). This raised new questions for us as a network: could we take strategies from one school and place them successfully in another? What did we have to take into consideration before this began to work?

The network also provided a social and supportive element. It was what one teacher described as a welcome 'pressure release', where there was an opportunity to offload anxieties and concerns about school. Sometimes these were funny and sometimes they were distressing; but, because the network had established a trusting climate at the inter-school meetings, colleagues were supportive, sympathetic and able to offer each other useful strategic and developmental responses to alleviate some of the pressures they faced.

At first I struggled to establish why this was so. But teachers were clear that there was no challenge to their school status and that they were in a situation of shared power, they controlled the agendas, they decided on the focus and the pace of the meetings, they raised what they wanted to raise, and did not raise what they did not want to. So control, power, focus, voice and choice were all cited as important qualities of the network that the teachers valued and strove to maintain.

The experience of knowledge-sharing led us to think further about how we could convey salient lessons to other schools. One network event was poster-based to capture key components of the projects, supported by a series of roundtable discussions on identified themes related to teaching and learning and the use of qualitative data-gathering instrumentation. We reported some of our findings in the local newsletter, we wrote articles for the local and national newspapers, and we considered what we might do to take the initiative forward. One school gained DfEE funding for a network link to an independent school; another used the same model of network to develop a new approach to parental and community liaison.

Perhaps most salient to our broader discussion of schools inside integrated learning systems was our recognition of how little opportunity the teachers had to meet inside school or between schools to do this type of work. This was despite its obvious developmental value for the individuals (we began to notice the 'ISIS effect', where staff involved – over 75 per cent of the team co-ordinators – gained promotion!) and the structural changes it brought to their schools, with perform-ance enhancement by students – no school in the initiative dropped in performance, while all but one improved and have continued to exceed previous best performance in GCSE grades and a wider range of more thorough and stimulating projects. The focus of ISIS, and its sustained attention on teaching and learning legitimized teachers' opportunities to take risks and to innovate; in a sense it made 'risk' safer because of the supportive nature of the network.

I concluded that schools had so little opportunity to do this type of work simply because it was groundbreaking. We had begun to encounter a process of working that changed the individualized school concept and offered something different, something that shifted the emphasis of learning towards shared enter-prise within individual units. I will return to this observation in Part 3.

OBSERVATIONS ARISING FROM THE ISIS PROJECT

Using mistakes as well as successes to inform the learning process

In the first year of the initiative we had to draw on what people from elsewhere could tell us about their schools improvement. By year two we had our own, local knowledge base. Teachers from the first cohort were invited to give a 'warts and all' description of their project activity in the year to the new intake to the ISIS initiative, and each September these stories continue to unfold as each school journey, year on year, is retold to a wider audience. Those teachers attending the ISIS meetings for the first time were shown how in many cases teachers had used mistakes and dilemmas as significant opportunities for leverage in school.

These observations ran counter-intuitive for many teachers, who felt at the start of the project that they had to have a coherent plan, that their procedures had to be clear and ready and that they had to avoid any hint of controversy. As we grew in confidence working within the cohort teams, teachers became more willing to discuss failure and challenge the methods that they were being encour-aged to use to inform and strategize for change. We grew to find that failure had its ups as well as its downs, although this realization was sometimes painful.

'Others may walk this way' – Making strategic choices more transparent

Early in the initiative a teacher brought in the following quote and we used it as a discussion point about choices we made in our improvement initiatives and the way in which those choices were interpreted by other colleagues.

> I believe that in our conscious life we are all midwives to reality. We are a bridge between the realm of potentiality and the world of actuality. Through our imaginations we are in touch with a plethora of possibility, yet in our focused thoughts we must choose one from

> the many. When we focus our attention on a situation or a problem we ... pluck one of a number of infinite number of routes and actualise it. Once it is actualised it can be measured and observed and we may discuss its properties ... the more of those properties we can get to know the closer we come to being in touch with the larger underlying reality. (Zohar and Marshall, 1993)

Often, in the ISIS initiative, participants brought to the table selected readings, strategies and examples of what had provoked and stimulated their work. I like to think that one of our great successes has been to focus teachers' attention on the possible links that exist between thought, selection and action. Sometimes we were able to show this through the salient messages in the research literature documenting other improvement projects (for example, see Louis and Miles, 1991; Hopkins, Ainscow and West, 1994; Dalin, 1993; Dalin and Rust, 1994; Stoll and Myers, 1998). To establish this way of working, the participants in the initiative

---

Success coming out of failure

In one school ISIS simply did not work. I felt that this was going to be the case during the first meeting I had with the school ISIS team. During a long discussion on matters related to change and planning of initiatives across multiple departments I suggested that they should play the long game and seek strategic activity that would change organizational teams, and that they should do this in collaboration with another school in the network. The team had different ideas and wanted short-term, almost off-the-peg, quick-fire solutions to a problem of under-performing boys. They most certainly did not want to share their successes with others.

The way that these teachers saw change ran completely counter to my own understanding and experience and what I valued in building learning teams. But in the spirit of the initiative I committed time to work with the school. These school visits continued to be both challenging and hostile territory. The school team and I had completely different viewpoints about how to influence and change teaching and learning. Our meetings sparked, disagreements continued, and ideas never seemed to develop. My records of the meetings still shout out to me the frustration experienced in those meetings. We covered the same ground each time, we argued over minutiae that seemed to be trivial and meaningless and to miss the chances to use the focus on the boys' under-performance to touch on teaching approaches, and perhaps on what the boys themselves thought of the teachers and the curriculum they were offered. Instead we developed a merit scheme. I left that school feeling I had let them down and that I had never really been given a chance to work constructively with them. I left the school at the end of the year and understood considerably more about issues of readiness for change. At a later network meeting the co-ordinator came to me and said that the school ISIS team had started to look at teaching and learning and had used a questionnaire developed by another school in the initiative to identify what the students thought of the styles of teaching being used in school.

---

were encouraged to keep a watchful eye on what colleagues in other improvement initiatives were saying about their work, and to confirm or counter the claims coming from elsewhere. We examined the implications and lessons from other project reports and attempted to identify from them what we could learn and use in each of the ISIS schools.

Our early forays into the uses and applications of improvement initiatives elsewhere taught us a great deal about the modelling of strategic approaches to change in schools. We found that a good deal of the work reported elsewhere was very hard to understand because the literature was from other school systems, which teachers felt represented other ways of approaching schooling. In the literature from the UK, teachers said that the interpretive choices schools had made – why they saw what they saw as a problem, why they took a particular developmental approach, and what they sought to achieve – were often not explained and remained opaque. Without these contextual features it was difficult to discover why the schools wanted to focus so much attention, for example, on what seemed to be 'one-off' gains such as improving borderline results from grade D to grade C, where there was little evidence that the school would glean from such activity any form of sustainable practice which could be replicated in later work with other cohorts. There may well have been fine reasons for their activity, but a lack of transparency meant that we felt, as travellers walking on similar ground, that we could not read their maps.

At a developmental level for the initiative we realized that this message was of significance to us. If we couldn't understand the practicalities of what was coming from improvement literature, we had to work hard to make sure that our own work was sufficiently transparent in intention and meaning to enable our colleagues in the ISIS initiative to gain a conceptual grasp of why, what, and how they were 'seeing' and 'doing' their improvement. This included working on how to represent thoughts, possible choices and subsequent actions to a wider audience.

Similarly, we found that there are many more 'grey' areas in improvement activity than the literature seems to want to report. Throughout the initiative things went wrong just as often as things went right. People had to cancel meetings, staff didn't get enough time to do what they wanted to do, the pressure of meeting deadlines for mandatory activity required by examinations boards skewed pre-planned time frames, staff gained promotion and left at critical moments in the plan. These factors all had an effect on how we now informed our work, how we talked about the initiatives as a process and how we informed and selected what to do, and why a particular action was selected. Increasingly, the school teams moved towards the development of strategic methods that could service sustained conversations on teaching and learning which could respond to the undulating nature of school life and be revisited and revised.

The importance of validating the grass-roots opinion

ISIS draws upon activities and approaches from colleagues in other projects and settings, but *not* at the cost of inhibiting local discussion on what 'improvement' might mean for the individual school and the people within it, even when the viewpoint might be quite different. In this way ISIS can be said to have made a stand to validate the local, grass-roots opinion of what seems to work. We have learnt that the careful selection of methods and the models, ideas and approaches used in order to introduce change do influence teachers' willingness to participate and to try and change practice. At our cost, in the early stages of the initiative, we pushed on what others were saying, rather than what we learnt, and I think we have identified that too great a homage to the canon of improvement literature, no matter how informed and illuminating, makes us subservient to it rather than to the need to inform the discretion of the local critical community in school. It says something about giving people a voice to legitimize an interpretation of the demands being made on their organization, and feeling that they can exercise power in the choices that they make to pursue their approaches.

In the ISIS initiative, the blend of urban deprivation, limited local prior experience of sustained improvement work in collaboration with external teams, and limited prior inter-school networking created a set of unique and challenging social, political and educational problems for us as a group to begin to unravel and understand. As the initiative has developed, so too has our conceptual approach to the challenge of school improvement in this setting. We have established a more consistent platform of understanding between schools through the networking process and we are in a position to be able to report to each other within the community of schools in the ISIS initiative more coherently and constructively. This has arisen because of a responsive method of approach from the external team, because the structure of the initiative has moved with the stated needs of the schools, and because we draw attention to the ways in which colleagues are framing their problems and responding strategically to them at each site.

Time frames: change and pace

In many 'modern' schools the early stages of an initiative see a desire to specify the 'results' and an attempt, in the developmental stage of the work, rapidly to establish a cause-and-effect set of steps through which change will happen according to a predetermined time scale. This had the effect of establishing some ISIS teams as clock-watchers eager to see if their efforts were showing evidence of having arrived at the desired point. The adverse effect of this was to take these teams' eyes off the emerging links between the separate initiatives that they had planned. Some opportunities were missed in the early stages of the initiative because of a lack of flexibility regarding remodelling, realigning and adapting as some of the initiatives evolved.

However, as the initiative's longer time frame began to seep into the experience of the team, discussion shifted to some of the seemingly slower, less immediately tangible activities, and it is these that seem to have been a lasting legacy of the initiative in schools and the ground of some important insights. In particular I noticed that as the teams began to look towards the longer-term impact of change their attention turned towards:

- the way change 'conversations' shifted from discussion about immediate response to identified problems to a consideration of what might be influencing the problem, and what series of approaches, when brought together, could form a more sustained response;
- the design of systemic reform aimed at identifying difference;
- the ways that data were analysed in different ways by different staff in order to create a 'hot-pot' of discussion points;
- the ways that the schools began to change organizational structure so as to open up debate across all layers of staff, rather than leaving strategic activity to senior managers;
- the way the plans began to evolve in one school rather than be predefined for the year;
- on a personal level, the way I began to see schools differently, necessitating a different conceptual shape to improvement that could configure the key constitutional features of the organization, and through which I could then begin to understand better the basis of the particular approaches the school was taking.

Of particular note were the following transitional themes:

- The move away from assuming that change is a simple process of cause and effect, towards a more complex understanding that tries to establish relationships between abstractions in the form of themes and emerging possibilities as well as planned intentions;
- less emphasis on a strict definition of the job of teaching and more on the multiple roles and the flexibility that learning support and teaching demand for oneself, colleagues and students;
- a move from the certainty of plans which formulate intentions as absolutes, towards a willingness to embrace a range of possible outcomes and to live with the results which are more responsive, case sensitive and emergent;
- an appreciation of the limitations of an individualistic way of operating, and an effort to develop a set of structures that builds on the support and experience of others in the form of both inter and intra school networks.

The core areas of transition outlined in Table 5.2 are excerpted from the school growth map shown in Chapter 4 (see Table 4.2, p. 57).

I have already described the following set of issues in Chapter 2, but I raise them again here because they tell us a lot about the important role that time plays in making improvement make personal and collective sense. They also speak of how change from one paradigm to another cannot be forced, but, like the summer, 'it does come. But it comes only to the patient' (Rilke, 1986).

- **Listening to local agendas:** This implies undermanagement rather than overmanagement of ideas in development. In periods of change in the ISIS initiative we recognized that it was necessary to allow space in network meetings and to

Table 5.2 *An indication of the trajectory of the core areas of transition*

	Ways of thinking (cognitive)	Ways of living and working (inter-personal)	Ways of seeing (intra-personal)	Seeking	Assumed underlying structure
Modern paradigm	Assumes cause and effect	Role-conscious		Concrete – certainty in outcomes	Individualistic
Beyond-modern transitions	Establishing relations between abstractions	Conscious of multiple role		Less than certain increasing willingness for flexibility	Networked

recognize the place of open discussion in school, so as to enable strategic conversations to emerge and activity to form rather than have an organizational pattern forced upon it too soon.

- **Designing in systems to tackle difference:** In ISIS we learnt that anyone can initiate strategic action and that schools cannot plan *when* strategies will emerge, they just will. What schools have to develop is the capacity to problematize difference and use it constructively within their local setting so that they can learn to 'hear one another' in the locality, raising issues about working with learners, and can be open to identifying what is happening and when it is working, even if that runs counter-intuitive to the norm of the organization.
- **Seeking patterns:** ISIS schools have developed approaches to data-gathering that enable staff to describe practice and subsequently to connect it with their colleagues' approaches in order to establish common patterns and themes. These have then been used to consider questions of consistency of approach and of difference, and to identify areas of concern.
- **Developing the ability to act and to choose not to act:** This emphasizes both the conscious and accidental/managed and unmanaged processes that schools adopt in order to enable the flow through the school of ideas that can inform them of the most suitable ways to move forward in their work. These might be deliberate, or they might not, but once they begin to matter, they become more formally structured into the school life.
- **A freeflowing and emergent approach to strategy:** We noticed in the ISIS schools a pattern of action, urgent in the early autumn and tending then to bed down until early spring, when there is another deliberate surge of activity; a final surge comes just at the start of the summer term. This is subliminally known by staff, and when they recognize it is happening in more overt ways they are in a position to use this observation to far greater effect. They can predict that they will innovate more, they will initiate trials and small-scale

'risk-taking' activity, and as a result school is more likely to be turbulent. They will be able to learn more about their own organizational learning patterns.

- **Recognizing the 'constitutional configuration':** ISIS helped me to understand when to intervene and when not to do so. This is about using established ways of working to best effect, and it is about formulating quite new approaches to lever innovation and dramatic shifts in organizational activity.

OTHER PRACTICAL OBSERVATIONS: 'PROCESSING' THROUGH EVENTS

There are some other practical messages arising from the ISIS initiative that serve as pointers on the improvement journey.

We remained committed to the insight that school improvement is a process and not an event (Fullan, 1991), but we began to consider whether school improvement that is operating on a threshold point such as that at the interface of modern to beyond-modern transitional and ecological paradigms is better conceptualized as both a process *and* an event. Our reasoning was that we found the 'events' of change in school provided staff with a focus from which an understanding of the supporting process could be described. We illustrated this through the use of 'change maps' (Clarke, 1996), where we encouraged co-ordinators to keep a diary of whatever they felt to be key moments of their ISIS initiative. As these maps developed, they provided the co-ordinator, the school team and the network meetings with a visual hook to hang discussion on, as well as a way of illustrating and illuminating patterns of activity in the school.

As ISIS was interested in facilitating cultural change as well as technical changes to the structure of the school, it was necessary to request a long-term commitment from the schools to the ISIS initiative, the minimum period of involvement being two years. In some cases these change maps provided a helpful means of capturing the undulating activity taking place in the form of a process/event register.

LOCATING PERSONAL AND ORGANIZATIONAL FEELING ABOUT PROPOSED AND ACTUAL CHANGE

Change maps provided one simple instrument for identifying, through record and discussion, indications of cultural change through differences in the staff response to, and uptake of, improvement activity. A second instrument we used was in the form of a response typology, designed to capture the 'mood' of staff in response to particular events and to serve as a device through which we could explore different scenarios for change and gain some sense of the likely response if we were to pursue them.

The process of gathering data on staff response to change events can be difficult. It is possible, particularly at the outset of a change process, that staff will

Table 5.3 *An example of a 'school change map' from an ISIS partner school*

Time	Issue	Process of activity	Links
Summer 1997	Identification of key theme: learning progression from end of KS3 to GCSE	Staff meeting – leading to identification of areas of concern	Data sets on GCSE and KS3 performance
Autumn 1997	'What will we look for?' Ideas generated at staff meeting about what we might look for to provide insights into what was influencing this performance	Whole staff discussion: teams established and feed back to ISIS group	School development plan; governors' meeting
	Themes identified: detention and referrals to academic remove; gender differences re: 'lunch-time detentions' during a collection period spanning one half term; attendance and punctuality; merits	Themes identified and resources gathered to inform the discussion	Departmental meetings focused on themes
	Questionnaire	Developed within the ISIS team and modified through departmental meetings	Outcomes shared with staff - modifications made and student groups identified
	Years 9 & 10 questionnaire	Students use the questionnaire	
Spring 1998	Responses to questionnaire	Analysis by ISIS team	Feedback of questionnaire to students and staff
	'Recommendations' and 'next steps' identified	Plan produced by ISIS team	Shared with staff
	Staff reflection on GCSE results	Whole school training day identifying themes	

Table 5.3 continued

	Reasons for under-performance focused upon in departmental teams	Discussion across departmental teams; themes reported to senior management team	
	'Characteristics of underachievers' identified, drawn from staff strategies found useful in improving performance of underachievers	Whole staff meeting and follow-up in departmental teams	To School Development Plan for coming year
Summer/ Autumn 1998	The Quality Learning Initiative	Staff training day	Connections with earlier data sets identified
	Outcomes analysed at different 'layers' of the school	Identify areas of concern/ strength	
	Whole school map	ISIS strategic suggestions	School Development Plan
	The outcomes of the Faculty Development plans	Targets set	
Spring 1999	Whole school issues identified	Links made with faculty plans	
	The progress report	Given to all staff – responses encouraged	
	An outline of progress made in implementing each priority	Requests for further information on teaching changes made to all staff	
Summer 1999	Identification of new/shared/tried methodologies	Resource book developed and shared across school, outlining all successfully identified teaching approaches	

t willing to share openly with colleagues for fear of
ıg to 'toe the line'. However, gathering data that can
ıd to negative and positive orientations of change is
ıe response typology enables data on staff response to
ıf desired, and we found it provided the ISIS teams with
plore change with both students and teachers. Using a
ponse (Clarke and Christie, 1997) we were able to map a
esponses to change. These were classed as:

ıange is of no use to me'
change might be of some use to me'
- Ac   ange is useful and I'll get involved'
- Creative.   v that we know what we can do, how can we develop it?'

These types of response can be analysed as follows:

- **Reactive response: 'This change is of no use to me'.** Change is often presented as a move towards 'best' practice. The reactive respondent is often thought of as a person who is unwilling to change. Reactive responses suggest a different view from that which is being presented by the change initiator. The initiating factor for a reactive response may be an external requirement, such as to administer and accept the results of an inspection, or it may be the response to an internal initiative promoting a collaborative approach to a behaviour policy. The principal point is that when teachers express their concerns in relation to the perceived event, invariably those teachers are in an adverse power relationship to the initiator. That is, the reactive agent is often seen by the initiator as negative and unwilling to change something which the initiator wants to see changed. This type of response is seen to be important, as it is a recurrent observation amongst some staff to some events and it often leads to increased consideration by other staff involved in order to clarify what they are doing or have done, and asking whether the action has or will have the effect that is claimed.
- **Engaging response: 'This might be of some use to me'.** In schools which were observed on the initial use of the instrument (Clarke, 1997), this response was typically demonstrated by a minority of staff, often senior in status, who felt that the event might have some school-wide benefit. In taking this stance the staff engage in an exploration of some of the features of the event which might serve to legitimize its use. During times of engagement there is often considerable unofficial discussion of the kind which explores the general 'feel' (Leithwood, 1994 and 1992) amongst staff for the event. 'What do you think about it?' 'Do you think we should?' are the types of questions being posed. Engaging responses appear to develop an undercurrent of attitudes to the event which establish a staff opinion on whether the event is likely to succeed.
- **Active response:'This is useful to me and I'll get involved'.** Active responses are those where staff believe that there is individual and collective merit in an event being followed. They are typified by practical questions such as 'How might we do this?', 'Who is going to do this?' The active responses are

important to team-building, leading to a more collaborative culture. Once an event is attempted successfully it provides an opportunity for a more rigorous involvement of staff to occur because those who were less convinced can see the practical benefits for their own involvement.

- **Creative response: 'Now we know what we can do, how can we develop it?'** Once a school staff has begun to feel confident in its interpersonal working to the extent where actions and events can be critically evaluated to identify their formative effect upon the organization, the staff move into a creative mode of response. This response allows staff to use events in order to inform their understanding of the change process as well as the outcomes or products of the event. During the creative phase a working meta-language is in operation between staff; it is not always spoken but is evident as an understanding of how things work in school and 'what will work well and what will not'. This understanding is established through the knowledge of successful ways of working that the staff have shared – in effect they 'see', 'live', 'work' and 'think' about improvement differently. When faced with a new initiative, staff have the capacity to understand the meaning behind the initiative and to relate it to other improvement initiatives. They collectively understand that they will have the voice to say what they want about the change and they are empowered to articulate their views.

The response taxonomy can be extended through the use of the matrix shown in Table 5.4, which was used when we found that we faced particularly difficult periods of staff unease at the reforms being attempted. Each staff member would indicate their present feelings on the matrix, and following analysis the ISIS team was then able to discuss the general trends indicated by the response matrix, and the problems the response matrix raised for the implementation of the change.

Whilst the main commitment of the ISIS initiative focused on teaching and learning, there were plenty of opportunities arising from this focus to enable staff to explore the underlying processes that were inhibiting and enhancing the capacity of staff and students to learn. The change mapping and response typologies supported these lines of inquiry alongside the use of questionnaires and interviews developed for use in specific projects. They added considerably to the tone of the activity taking place in schools: rather than accepting straightforward and clear-cut approaches, some schools 'learnt' to live with greyer, less certain approaches to change, and were developing a more sensitized set of strategies to inform and guide their intuitions.

The process/event discussions facilitated questions concerning the link between practical matters of teaching and learning with a broader purpose of school. We spent some of the network time asking: What are learning schools? What do they do? How do they differ from what already exists? Why are they worth striving for? What would we look for in them to indicate that learning is happening at personal and organizational levels? Bringing these questions into the school improvement discussions served to offer a longer-term purpose to the improvement agenda and has widened the brief, so that attention was not merely focused on making structural changes to timetables, groups of students and curriculum schedules, but allowed staff to consider whether the organizational culture and

Table 5.4 *Eight stages of change linked to personal response*

	Stage 1	Stage 2	Stage 3	Stage 4	Stage 5	Stage 6	Stage 7	Stage 8
	feeling unsettled	denying/ resisting	facing the present situation	letting go into the unknown	envisioning the desired future	exploring new options	committing to action	integrating the change
Response type	reactive	reactive	engaged	active	active	creative	creative	creative
What I do	I admit dissatisfaction	I recognize my resistance or denial for what it is	I face my situation realistically	I grieve for the losses associated with saying goodbye, including what I lost by hanging on too long to an inappropriate situation	I can visualize what I want or how I want to be in the future	I can explore new options I have envisioned myself, and experiment with new behaviours and feelings	I can choose the options that seem most appropriate	I can integrate the new quality or behaviour into my life, bringing more of my whole self to the party so that I operate at a higher level of complexity and maturity

Table 5.4 *continued*

What I feel about this	I can feel that this is not right	I can overcome or manage my fears	I am non-judgemental	I can feel sadness, ability to accept uncertainty	I know what I want	I can take risks	I can make decisions and eliminate options	I allow my various traits and impulses to communicate with one another; ability to feel and act on more than one impulse at once in an integrated way
What I need to let go of	an attachment to always feeling fine or in control	denial or resistance	an old picture of who I am or how things should be	the need to know what I want and where I am going	the safety of sticking to what is familiar	having to be good at everything that I do	other alternatives, the need to keep options open	the sense of loss associated with choosing this instead of that; the need to have the perfect answer
What I need to learn	I can handle pain/discomfort	I understand how my denial/resistance is an attempt to protect myself	I can move ahead into the unknown without triggering more denial and resistance	I can handle not knowing where I am heading or how things will turn out	I trust that something new and more appropriate emerges out of the chaos	I am open to new ways of being and doing things	I can envision something new and make it a reality	I can continue to learn and grow

Source: Adapted from Campbell, 1996.

structures of their schools and classrooms were inhibiting or enabling real change to occur that shifted understandings and practice.

CONCLUDING THOUGHTS ABOUT THE ISIS INITIATIVE

The best way of understanding ISIS is perhaps to put it into the broader context of improvement taking place in the latter part of the 1990s, and to see it inside the transformations taking place in political, social and educational arenas. The receptivity of some of the schools to undertaking a radically different conceptual approach to change, and their willingness to share their reform agendas openly with other schools within a locality served as a reminder that the 'individualistic' culture was not the only way of improving schools. Indeed, the pursuit of internal reforms raised the possibility of schools establishing important connections with other agencies in the locality. In recognizing this possibility, we began to identify the mutual benefits gained by looking at shared themes, where a community of schools was often struggling with very similar practical and conceptual problems concerned with change.

ISIS had its problems, all essentially human rather than system-related, but nevertheless real. We felt a shared frustration at the limited amounts of discussion and development time; we had frustrations about colleagues' seemingly endless unwillingness to participate constructively in debate; we had pressures from managers bent on quick fixes; and we had problems with new buildings, old buildings, staff changing jobs, teams reforming half-way through the projects. However, what remained at the core of the activity was the importance given to listening and constructively receiving the opinions of people, asserting the dignity of human relationships in a learning-orientated community, and how this can be seen as an active realization of democracy. ISIS gave each teacher in each school an opportunity to participate in their daily lives through a shared effort that was at once redesigning processes of understanding how their schools learnt, and redesigning how their teachers taught. It began a transformational journey, it began to create its own pathway to the learning school.

KEY ISSUES AND IDEAS IN THIS CHAPTER

- We set out to design a system of support and critique that could be focused on internal school activity and subsequently shared at intra-school events. Conceptually this initiative had a transformative rationale, although this understanding grew out of the initiative rather than existing because of it. The main thrust of the transformation was from schooling, towards a redesigned practice of learning.
- We developed this system according to some basic principles of operation that were learning-orientated.
- We designed a simple and robust model of support which committed all participants to the art and practice of sustained conversation through a busy

agenda of activity, meetings and intra-school events, where the participants were expected to report findings and shared instrumentation with colleagues from other schools.

- As the initiative developed we recognized a series of beneficial features emerging. These were described by teachers involved as being of value to them and to their school colleagues. These features included:
  - The mutual gains of networking: we learnt that shared knowledge became more than a commodity and was a way of establishing a group identity.
  - Mistakes as well as successes were part of the process of learning: the denial of failure inhibited some projects' capacity to redesign and remodel. As the trust between teams developed, so too did their willingness to share the failures and to seek alternative suggestions for their developmental approaches.
  - It was important to try and make our work transparent: this led us into conversations about how to use other schools' materials. As we developed our approaches to improvement, we began to experiment with approaches that other schools had taken and found that taking them at face value did not help. It was necessary to modify, to mould ideas into the shapes that best suited the unique nature of the receiving culture. This had an interesting effect of leading internal, school investigations into a wider range of data sources than those they normally drew upon, such as student voice and parental opinion, and this therefore created new channels of information on what was working and what was not.
  - We learnt what it was like to create a knowledge-generating community and how this created an energy of its own, where people grew in confidence and creativity in their improvement approaches.
  - We found that different types of improvement reflect different views of time: short-term solutions sometimes worked when schools needed a morale boost, but they had to be complemented with broader and more robust thoughts about where things might be moving in the longer term. This raised the significance of local voice in making choices about the pace and nature of change in an improvement environment which was measured inside mandated parliamentary periods.
  - We found that difference mattered, even where schools sought similar aims in terms of pupil performance outcomes. Their different approaches served to amplify the importance of understanding the organizational self and not avoiding difference and the potential difficulties that this could raise on school sites.
  - We became more 'pattern' focused in the school and network meetings: teachers noted themes, approaches, 'typical' responses that they were finding from colleagues in school, and used these to explore strategic understanding and establish links between different improvement activities.
  - Strategic learning led to changes in the intervention approaches taken: some teachers were more willing to allow a change process to evolve, instead of wanting to continue to take measures to identify progress. This was taken as a riskier but beneficial approach, as it began to show signs of a new way of

seeing improvement in more compound ways which linked processes and events more closely together and prompted innovative ways of gathering data to inform colleagues of their responses towards changes taking place.

- Finally, we can reflect on the meaning of this initiative inside the wider socio-political climate of reform. It has many of the trappings of other improvement activities taking place in the same time frame. However, the attention to the inter-school network puts it on a trajectory into the systemic ecological paradigm of a learning school and has initiated change discourses that go beyond the individualization of schools, offering some pointers towards the integrative potential of a learning community.

Chapter 6

A Journey into Learning

From time to time, [the] tribe [gathered] in a circle. They just talked and talked and talked, apparently to no purpose. They made no decisions. There was no leader. And everybody could participate. There may have been wise men or women who were listened to a bit more – the older ones- but everybody could talk. The meeting went on, until it finally seemed to stop for no reason at all and the group dispersed. Yet after that, everybody seemed to know what to do, because they all understood each other so well. Then they could get together in smaller groups and do something or decide things.
David Bohm, *On Dialogue*

In this chapter I want to describe one school's journey of learning. I have maintained a close link with this school over a three-year period, during which it has initiated a comprehensive range of developments which have begun to transform the culture from one operating along the lines of individualized reform to a more integrated, systemic approach.

To provide a structure to the chapter I will describe the school and then proceed to illustrate, through a series of brief cameos and data sets, some of the approaches the staff took in developing their understanding of what really mattered to their school. At points along the journey I will indicate key issues which relate to the level of development that the school was demonstrating. I will reflect in the subsequent discussion about the way that the school is thinking, living and working.

EVOLUTION TO A DATA-RICH CLIMATE USED TO INFORM STRATEGIC APPROACHES TO LEARNING

The context

The school is a popular and oversubscribed secondary school with approximately 700 pupils on roll. Public examinations over the period 1994–1997 had shown a steady improvement, with a significant rise between 1996 and 1997. A significant difference had been observed between the results achieved by boys and by girls. In September 1995 a working party of five staff was set up to investigate improving examination results. Over a two-year period the group made a number of recommendations on strategies that could be adopted to improve the results of all pupils, and boys in particular.

The focus and rationale of the initiative

I began working in the school at a point where the first learning-oriented activities had begun and staff were gathering information on student performance, attendance, merit systems and punctuality at school. Prior to my involvement, there had been a series of external reports and consultancies linked with the school, which had all been briefed to focus attention on boys' under-performance.

Whilst there was a range of interesting comments and ideas suggested by the outsiders, one significant theme seemed to raise itself time after time. The theme was that of managing behaviour. In my capacity as consultant to a larger project within the LEA I was asked to come in and develop this line of work with staff. This was interesting in itself, because I really have no experience at all in the area of behaviour management; but, on listening to what senior staff began telling me, I admit that I felt very uneasy about the form of advice that the school had been given. I spent time talking to the staff about what they saw as the real issues related to under-performance, and began to feel that they had been pushed down a particular path towards providing a managed 'solution'.

My strong initial response to what I was presented with was that, somehow, dealing with the matter as a technical one of managing behaviour simply avoided some of the deeper and more significant features of the debate that staff were having amongst themselves about performance, motivation and learning. Watching these same teachers teaching and in their own ways trying to carry through with the boys themselves this debate about performance served to confirm my feelings. There was an apparent distance between the teaching of the subject and the connection with the learners as people struggling to learn new concepts, ideas and ways of seeing and thinking. I reflected back on what the consultants and advisers had done. They had undertaken reviews of incidents of indiscipline, looked at the frequency of these, and looked at which subjects seemed to have the greatest problems of under-performance and its associated difficulties with behaviour and lack of interest. All of this work had served to redefine a problem which had somehow emerged as one related to control and a challenge to teacher and school authority. I felt that this was a mistake and that the approach was acting as a blinker to the central matter of learning and how the students were being encouraged – and discouraged – to learn. This case study developed as a result and is, I believe, indicative of a school slowly gaining the confidence to trust its own judgement and inform its own developmental objectives.

PHASE 1: SEEKING CERTAINTY

The original focus for the school ISIS project was raising the attainment of boys as measured by Key Stage 3 (KS3) and GCSE results. In the school's Annual Report prior to Ofsted inspection in January 1997, the difference between boys' and girls' attainment at GCSE was highlighted: 'Girls' attainments were much higher than boys' at age 16. At this school the boys' deficit in comparison with girls' is amongst the highest in the country.' It therefore came as little surprise to the staff, following a very positive inspection of the school, that raising the attainment of boys was targeted as a key area for improvement by the senior management team and governing body, in which they should:

> Give an even greater urgency to raising boys' attainments through a range of strategies:

- Setting up clearly defined systems for monitoring progress against prior attainment data;
- Monitoring attitudes and the impact of school policies (e.g. behaviour for learning) on boys' self-esteem and aspirations;
- Establishing strong early links between GCSE, subject departments and the tutorial programme to challenge and raise aspirations.

The 1997 GCSE results saw a significant closing of the gap between boys and girls. The school was eager to identify reasons for this and to explore strategies which would further improve boys' attainment at KS3 and GCSE. This led the senior management team to the conclusion that they needed much more information to draw upon in order to begin to make strategic decisions about the nature of the improvement activity that might best be undertaken in response to what they were observing in their outcome performance results.

Key issues:

- Externally identified issues and points of action

- Senior management team making strategic decisions about approaches to take in response

---

Initiating the project

A working party of teaching staff was created to take a lead role in finding out what differences existed in boys' and girls' performance and general activity in school. The aim was to establish a cross-curricular group consisting of staff with a range of responsibilities and experience, who would then take to their colleagues the message of the inclusiveness of the improvement work being attempted.

The working party consisted of:

- ISIS Project Co-ordinator
- Maths Curriculum Co-ordinator
- Headteacher
- Head of Faculty (English and MFL)
- Head of Faculty (Arts and Movement)
- Year 8 Co-ordinator
- Year 9 Co-ordinator
- Year 10 Co-ordinator
- Teachers from Geography, Science departments

- Equal Opportunities Co-ordinator

This team met once per half-term during the school year (six times yearly) to discuss and plan the detail of strategic initiatives. Members of the team, either individually or in pairs, also took part in data collection and analysis and the presentation of findings at whole staff INSET (In-Service Education and Training). Individual members of the team also took responsibility for overseeing particular initiatives during the year and acted as a link to the ISIS project in their own subject areas.

An initial decision was made by the team to collect and analyse as many forms of data as the staff felt was reasonably possible, and to use these data as a starting set by means of which they might then be in a position to inform strategic activity. After consultation with staff at a staff meeting for the whole school, the following data sources were identified and pursued as possible indicators which could lead staff to further knowledge about what was happening in school and could perhaps inform their response.

- Progression from end of KS3 to GCSE for the pupils who had left in Summer 1997
- Lunchtime detentions, after-school detentions and referrals to academic remove
- Attendance and punctuality
- Award of merits

A half-day training session was planned at the end of the first half term (Autumn). The purpose was to launch the improvement project school-wide, to inform staff of the initial consultative stages of the project, and to ask staff (in faculty groups) to reflect on the most recent set of GCSE results in teaching teams.

Key issues:

- A core team is formed

- Purposeful attention to data-led inquiry

- Individuals take responsibility for different aspects of the initiative

- Consultation with staff

- Indicators identified

The knowledge-generating school: drawing on an 'internal' analysis of data

The ISIS project encouraged schools to inform their improvement approaches through the uses of data, be it qualitative or quantitative. During the Summer term (1997) ISIS working party members spent a considerable amount of time collecting and analysing data. The purpose was to identify significant gender differences in attainment, behaviour, attendance, punctuality and attitudes to school. The results of the data analysis were discussed at length within the working party and then presented to the whole staff during INSET in September at the start of the term.

A summary of key issues arising from the data analysis is outlined in the following pages.

School-developed data sets

Data set 1: Progression from end of KS3 to GCSE
Data set 2: Detention and referrals to academic remove
Data set 3: Attendance and punctuality
Data set 4: Merits
Data set 5: Interview with Year 10 students
Data set 6: Year 9 Questionnaire
Data set 7: Staff reflection on GCSE results
Data set 8: Reasons for under-performance
Data set 9: Characteristics of underachievers
Data set 10: Strategies found to be useful in improving performance of underachievers
Data set 11: Quality and learning
Data set 12: Outcomes analysed at different 'layers' of the school
Data set 13: The faculty development plans
Data set 14: Whole school issues
Data set 15: Identification of new/shared/tried methodologies

Data set 1: Progression from end of KS3 to GCSE

What differences were identifiable in the performance of boys and girls, and was this a single-subject effect or did it demonstrate a broader pattern of performance?

English

It was found that a greater proportion of girls progressed to higher GCSE grades from SATs levels 5 and 6.

	SAT LEVEL 5–GCSE B or C	SAT LEVEL 6–GCSE A* to C
Girls	46%	100%
Boys	29%	88%

Mathematics

Here a greater proportion of girls progressed to higher grades from SATs levels 4 and 5. No significant difference was noted in progression from level 6.

	SAT LEVEL 4-GCSE C	SAT LEVEL 5–GCSE B
Girls	14%	23%
Boys	6%	6%

Science

Again a higher proportion of girls progressed to grade C from Level 5. There was no significant difference at level 6.

	SAT LEVEL 5-GCSE C
Girls	62%
Boys	41%

These data showed evidence of greater progression by girls from all levels of ability in school. It also indicated that, at the end of KS3, the highest attaining pupils were boys. However, at GCSE, with one exception, the highest attaining pupils were all girls.

The results of this analysis indicated strongly to the team that girls were learning at a different rate to boys from end of KS3 to GCSE. Moreover, girls were outperforming boys at all levels of ability. Staff decided that they needed to investigate the causes of this and apply the findings.

Data set 2: Detention and referrals to academic remove

Are boys more likely to get into trouble in school and initiate sanctions?

Acting on guidance from the senior management team, the ISIS team searched to find out what numbers of pupils were being placed on detention (a time sanction) and how this varied year by year and by gender (Table 6.1). The working party found that all year groups had significantly higher numbers of boys than girls being placed in detentions (both at lunchtime and after school). In years 8 and 11 in particular, a small number of pupils was identified as consistent 're-offenders' and accounted for a large proportion of detentions given.

These data were shared with teaching staff at a staff meeting. Following discussion it was decided that all staff would investigate further the reasons why boys and girls were being put in detention. More detailed analysis, carried out during the second term, indicated significantly higher numbers of boys being put into detention for poor behaviour in all year groups.

The discussion based on this detailed analysis prompted a second whole school investigation which explored the reasons why staff had put pupils in detention. The information which emerged is summarized in Table 6.2.

Across all year groups, the overwhelming reason for imposing detention was student behaviour thought unacceptable by the teacher. This information was stored for future use by the team.

Data set 3: Attendance and punctuality

Do boys attend school as regularly as girls in our school? Do boys get to school on time?

The proportions of boys and girls achieving 100 per cent attendance and 100 per cent punctuality over the first-half term were monitored (Tables 6.3, 6.4). The attendance figures indicated little difference between boys and girls, with higher proportions of boys achieving 100 per cent attendance in Years 9 and 10.

Table 6.1 *Gender Differences in lunchtime detentions during a collection period spanning one half-term*

	Number of occasions	Percentage of total	No. of pupils	Total number of pupils in year group
Year 7	28 occasions when boys were in detention 8 occasions when girls were in detention	77 23	26 6	160
Year 8	82 occasions when boys were in detention 30 occasions when girls were in detention	73 27	40 15	140
Year 9	94 occasions when boys were in detention 28 occasions when girls were in detention	67 33	40 20	128
Year 10	59 occasions when boys were in detention 27 occasions when girls were in detention	63 37	26 15	144
Year 11	65 occasions when boys were in detention 28 occasions when girls were in detention	60 40	29 19	126

Table 6.2 *Reasons for sanctions being imposed on students*

Reason for detention	Y7 Boy	Y7 Girl	Y8 Boy	Y8 Girl	Y9 Boy	Y9 Girl	Y10 Boy	Y10 Girl	Y11 Boy	Y11 Girl	Totals
Behaviour	18	0	24	5	15	9	24	2	9	1	107
Lateness	9	0	1	0	2	0	0	1	0	0	13
Homework	0	1	2	2	9	4	0	0	0	0	18
Equipment	2	0	3	1	3	3	0	0	3	1	16
Work rate	0	0	4	0	1	1	0	0	4	2	12
Missed previous detention	0	0	1	0	0	2	0	0	0	0	3
Totals	29	1	35	8	30	19	24	3	16	4	169

Table 6.3 *Percentage of pupils achieving 100% attendance*

	Boys (%)	Girls (%)	Number in year group
Year 7	57	54	160
Year 8	39	34	140
Year 9	27	18	128
Year 10	58	43	144
Year 11	28	32	126

Table 6.4 *Percentage of pupils achieving 100% punctuality*

	Boys (%)	Girls (%)	Number in Year group
Year 7	43	48	160
Year 8	42	39	140
Year 9	37	30	128
Year 10	28	26	144
Year 11	16	24	126

Figures for 100 per cent punctuality showed very little difference between the genders but did indicate that punctuality worsens as pupils get older.

Staff analysis of the data concluded that there were no significant differences in attendance and punctuality figures. However, they were concerned to note the increasingly poor punctuality in higher year groups.

This prompted discussion amongst teachers of the older students of the need for more careful monitoring of punctuality and to target students with poor punctuality records so as to commit them to better attendance.

Data set 4: Merits

Do students respond positively to awards?

The team gathered information on the number of merits teachers gave to each year group. Analysis of merits awarded for good work indicated that fewer merits were awarded to pupils as they progressed to higher year groups. This finding was in keeping with what other schools in the ISIS project were finding when the co-ordinator presented interim findings at the ISIS network meeting. There was some evidence to suggest that girls were gaining more merits than boys in Years 7 and 8. However, in Years 9, 10 and 11 there was very little difference between boys and girls.

Merits were apparently valued by pupils in Years 7 and 8, where students saw them as a status indicator. However, from Year 9 onwards the award of merits decreased significantly as 'public' recognition of achievement was seen as counterproductive by some students. There was also some anecdotal evidence to suggest that the award of a merit was seen as a 'stigma' by older pupils. The perception amongst some staff was that merits were not valued by older pupils, so there was little point in awarding them.

It was decided that the school needed to investigate alternative merit or reward structures, especially for pupils in upper school.

Key issues:

- A range of data sets was identified, questions were proposed and evidence gathered

- The team analysed and then informed all staff of the findings

- Discussions took place on the implications of the data

- Actions were decided upon some of the findings, other findings resulted in no action

---

PHASE 2: IDENTIFYING NEW POSSIBILITIES

Whilst the first phase focused on data sets which in the main confirmed what staff already knew, the second phase introduced data collection which extended the possibility of new insights through investigations into the personal responses of students, discussion and debate amongst staff of what students said, and a revisiting of data sets linked to exam performance with different questions driving the investigations.

Three specific activities took place.

- A series of interviews with Year 10 students;
- A survey of the attitudes of Year 9 students to school and a review of the key issues arising;
- Revisiting the GCSE results in the light of what the interviews and survey raised.

Data set 5: Interview with Year 10 students

What do students think about school? In what areas of their learning would they want further assistance?

A group of twenty boys was selected by staff as a representative sample of the ability range of boys in the year group. The boys were invited to attend a twenty-minute interview with me in my role as project consultant. The staff had already structured a series of prompting questions which were to be loosely adhered to as a means of providing some structure to the discussion. These questions concerned school, learning and the support that the boys felt they were getting in their learning. The questions were given to the boys before they came to the interview, and they were encouraged to talk with their friends and parents to inform their views.

All but one of the boys came to the interview and spoke quite openly about how they felt about their own learning and about their experiences of teachers in the school. A week later, following some initial analysis of the responses, I returned to the school and spent an afternoon with the entire group of boys. During this second session we discussed some of the themes that had emerged from the interviews. Further themes were identified and others clarified.

The outcomes of the group discussion were then cross-referenced with the individual interviews and all the findings were reported to the whole staff, then shared with the boys and finally the whole year. Staff also related these findings to their own faculty development plans and for the support for learning in the year.

The following points emerged from the interviews:

When learning worked well, the boys felt that learning was interesting and that they were succeeding
Factors contributing to this were:

1. Teachers are interested in boys as learners:
   - Listen to their opinions
   - Respond positively to their ideas
   - Establish and maintain a sense of order
   - Talk to them about their learning
   - Make suggestions, both spoken and written, to support their learning

- Are patient, calm, committed to support them as learners.

2. The presentation of the required work is clear:
   - Is well structured
   - Offers a variety of ways to respond or, over a period of time, will explore a variety of approaches
   - Links one set of activities to the next so that connections can be made
   - Is well explained

3. The method of teaching is stimulating. Preferred styles of learning would seem to be:
   - Practical tasks
   - Group activity
   - Discussion
   - Constructing own notes
   - Small working groups with teacher input

4. The follow-up is consistent across departments:
   - Homework, when set, is followed up in class
   - The homework is thoughtfully put together so as to relate to the session in school, but is also interesting developmental work
   - Homework is marked
   - The follow-up allows teacher/learner to have a discussion when needed on aspects of the work that were difficult or not understood

When learning breaks down, they felt that they were not enjoying the work

The boys' response here was something of a mirror image of the first set of points, in particular:

- Peer pressure: pressure from friends to mess about
- Group size: classes are too large and lead to distractions and less personal attention
- Teacher attitude:
  - Where the teachers focus only on certain pupils
  - Where teachers 'misused' the detention procedure
  - Where teachers were difficult to get in touch with
  - Where teachers didn't follow through on homework and practical to theory sessions
  - Where teachers didn't provide a structure to assist them in planning for learning

Preparation for Year 10 and Year 11 from lower school

There was a feeling that Year 10 had been considerably harder than they had expected, in particular with regard to raised expectations arising from:

- The increased amounts of homework
- The increased demands of coursework
- The preamble in Years 7–9 in leading up didn't prepare them for changing demands in the form of study that they needed to undertake

The boys suggested the following possible responses to these problems:

- To introduce a 'coursework' style of working earlier in school
- To develop a study skills programme to support and equip them with some generic approaches to study that would then be used in class by teachers
- To develop better links across the years and (my words) consider the progression (their words) the steps between years and subjects

Individual/personal study time

Boys said that they would like:

- More personal/quiet study time allocated
- Tutorial time used to talk with teachers instead of being taken up in writing
- Each lesson to have a plenary point that revises key issues covered
- Group study time to be supported by teachers' input to discuss successful study approaches in the subjects
- Increased access to teachers on a 1:1 basis outside of class. This is a very interesting point, as it came up in every one of the interviews. Boys were very aware of peer pressure and felt that asking the teacher was not always possible within the classroom setting

Data set 6: Year 9 questionnaire

What do students in this year group think about school? In what areas of their learning would they want further assistance?

A questionnaire was devised by the team and distributed to all pupils in Year 9. The questionnaire was completed inside school time, and students were informed that this would be a valuable addition to the staff efforts to improve the quality of learning support. The questionnaire asked for responses to eleven sections, as follows:

- General comments about school
- Pupils' feelings about lessons that they attended
- Pupils' perceptions of parents' views of their learning
- Pupils' perceptions of teachers
- Pupils' perceptions of teacher expectations of their work
- Pupils' opportunity/uptake of talking one-to-one with teachers
- Pupils' comments about the general level of education they felt they received from the school
- Pupils' response to careers guidance
- Pupils' personal comments on improvements in school
- Pupils' areas of concern in school
- Pupils' future plans post-school

The following key issues were identified from the questionnaire:

- General attitudes to school of both boys and girls were very positive

- A significant proportion of boys (39%) acknowledged that they only worked hard in some lessons
- A much smaller proportion of boys than girls stated that their parents always checked homework
- Around two-fifths of all pupils said few teachers praised their work, efforts or ongoing activity
- Approximately one-fifth of students felt teachers' expectations were low
- A high proportion of boys (36%) and girls (48%) had not had opportunities for one-to one discussion with their form tutor
- Approximately one-quarter of pupils wanted better careers information and guidance

Data set 7: Staff reflection on GCSE results

Is there a difference in the performance of boys and girls?

Following these interviews and questionnaires, the staff met in faculty groups and were asked to reflect again on the GCSE results and to focus on any marked gender differences in attainment they observed. Their findings are summarized in Table 6.5.

Table 6.5 *Identification of gender differences in attainment as shown by GCSE results*

YES		NO
Business Studies	more girls achieving A*–C	Physical Education (PE) Studies
Geography	boys achieving better results than girls	Drama
Religious Education (RE)	girls achieving higher results	Art
French	only 4 boys achieved A*–C	Music
Science	more girls than boys achieving B, C	History
Mathematics	no comment given	

At this point the team felt that they needed to reflect on what these different data sets were beginning to tell them. In doing this, they formulated some links between the sets which led them to want to develop further investigations into the matter of under-performance and its link with teaching and learning.

> **Key issues:**
>
> - There was a different orientation in the investigations, from areas of certainty – what staff already knew and needed confirmation of – to areas which they could use to inform where they moved to next
>
> - The involvement broadened the range of data collection instruments that the team developed, and the people involved – both students and outside 'critical' friends
>
> - There was an increase in the use of the data in smaller teams closer to the teaching and learning interface
>
> - Consultation on specific questions indicated a differentiated pattern of performance against subjects and prompted debate on how to proceed and how to intervene

PHASE 3: COMPLEX FORMULAS

Data set 8: Reasons for under-performance

You have read what some of our students think about school and learning. What do you think contributed to under-performance?

The staff were asked by the team to discuss in their teaching teams within faculties any issues which they felt were compelling reasons for the under-performance of boys relative to girls. These are summarized in Table 6.6.

Data set 9: Characteristics of underachievers

Describe an 'underachieving' student.

Each teaching team was asked by the ISIS team to identify any attributes that they felt were characteristic of an underachieving pupil. A brief synopsis of the replies is listed here:

- Failure to produce homework*
- Failure to meet deadlines
- Forgetting equipment
- Partial completion of work
- Lack of revision
- Lack of depth when completing exam questions
- Poor organizational skills*
- Good orally but poor written work*
- Poor attendance/punctuality
- Failure to copy up work when absent
- Over-confidence and complacency*
- Lack of concern over quality*
- Laziness

Table 6.6 *Reasons given by staff for students' under-performance*

Subject	Reasons for under-performance
Arts and Movement Faculty	Results very dependent on ability of cohort group opting for subject
Geography	Able boys produce very good coursework. Boys take more risks in answering questions on new topics
Religious Education	Girls spend more time on coursework. Boys better at answering knowledge-based questions but not good at evaluation
Technology	Different cultural expectations from boys and girls. Boys are not concerned about quality whereas girls strive for quality. Differing organizational skills
French	Seen as a female-dominated subject? Staffing? Teacher/learning styles. Boys fail to see point of learning a language
Science	Girls have different expectations/work ethic. Girls prefer theoretical work whereas boys prefer practical tasks. Girls have more mature attitude to studies

- Poor presentation
- Lack of pride
- Low self-esteem
- Immaturity
- Concern over image (peer pressure)*
- Behind with coursework
- Lack of interest in work
- Poor attitude to work
- Possible problems at home
- No male role model*

* Highlighted by some subject teachers as particular characteristics of boys.

This information was distributed to all teaching faculties in the school. Staff were asked to respond to the material by indicating those areas they felt they needed to focus on and add to their repertoire of teaching strategies. A feature of the thinking being shared between teaching teams concerned early identification procedures, which were formulated and passed up to the senior management team to develop as policy documents.

Data set 10: Strategies found to be useful in improving performance of underachievers

What do you do, in your teaching, to improve the performance of the underachieving student?

Having established a list of characteristics of under-performance, the staff in each teaching team were asked to indicate strategies which they had found successful in responding to some of these characteristics. A substantial base of information was gathered, and the following list shows some of the teaching strategies found to be useful in supporting underachieving students.

- Boys need greater support/structure. More clearly defined tasks to progress with coursework
- Seating plans: boy/girl, high/low achiever. Seating plans were found to be very effective in a number of subject areas
- Use of praise. Boys prefer this to be done one-to-one and not publicly
- Use of certificates
- Speaking to parents frequently, informally as well as formally
- Use of display work to indicate high-quality/exemplary work and work in progress
- Set interim deadlines to ensure final deadlines are met
- Comparison of standards
- Use of revision and tests to motivate
- One-to-one discussion; negotiation
- Use of surprise tests to combat over-confidence
- Boys need to see validity of tests if they are to make an effort for them
- Boys appear to learn better from discussion than from written work
- Low-ability boys enjoy being praised in front of others
- Ensure boy/girl balance when asking for volunteers
- Direct encouragement to individuals
- Closer monitoring of project work
- Year 9 and lower ability groups – use targets
- Review methodology of modular courses so that more choice is available
- Need for finite activities for some boys – seeing the end point
- Target setting
- Formative marking
- Continue to ask the pupils what they want

These strategies were put together into a resource pack and discussed at three strategic layers of the school: team, department and whole staff meeting. At the staff meeting considerable debate emerged and spread from the formal meetings, into corridors and car parks.

The core of the discussions was whether responses would be linked to the attributes, because it was evident that different staff had different approaches to the same pupil response. But there was also emergent discussion about how the project's decision-making should now proceed if it was to have an impact.

Review and reflection on progress

The vast amount of information that had been examined and debated across school prompted a decision by the team to stop and reflect on what they had learnt so far as a school and, also, what they should do next.

From the team's analysis of the outcome material developed and the responses they were getting to the consultation, discussion and developmental processes being used, a series of new questions emerged. The main focus of staff attention was now much more closely fixed on the teaching and learning taking place in the different classrooms, teaching teams and faculties. It was clear that the staff had enjoyed the opportunity to explore common themes, and the fourth phase of the project provided a chance to focus more productively on exactly what teachers were doing and how well students were responding to this.

Key issues:

- The orientation of the initiative began to turn slowly towards teachers' inquiry into learning about their own approaches to teaching

- Listening to students had initiated new aspects of inquiry

- Staff maintained an 'up-beat' response to the work, it was at a pace they felt was manageable, and it was driven by their own emerging knowledge base

- Review continued to inform and illuminate the thinking of the team

- Some concerns were emerging about where the initiative might go next. For example, should there be a consistent approach to tackling issues that were identified, or should an effort be made to maintain case-sensitive responses?

PHASE 4: STEERING A NEW COURSE

Following discussions within the Senior Management Team, the ISIS Working Party and after reviewing the results of the data analysis with outside advisers and the project consultant, it was decided that the next stage of the project would seek to involve at all times all staff, individually and collectively, in reviewing successful teaching and learning strategies.

The senior management felt strongly that there needed to be renewed clarity of objectives in the initiative, as the original focus had begun to evolve. The initiative was:

- To arrive at a consensus on the factors which contribute to quality learning;
- To encourage cross-curricular discussion and sharing of experience;
- To promote the sharing of good practice;
- To review teaching and learning strategies in the classroom;
- To implement new strategies and monitor their effectiveness in raising levels of attainment.

An indication of the significance of the focus on learning came in the renaming of the School Development Plan as a School Improvement Plan, with the first priority being the improvement of learning. Learning was conceptualized as having to occur at three levels to be seen to make a real impact:

- whole school level amongst staff members,
- teams of teachers at different 'layers' of the school – heads of facullty or departmental teams, subject teams;
- class level with pupils.

The work of the initiative became more interconnected at this point; a series of parallel investigations took place and each was used to inform the wider 'quality learning' debate. Some of the investigations tried to maintain a link between the personal work of the teacher and the wider agenda in the minds of all faculty heads – how can we transfer the areas of expertise of individual teachers for the benefit of all staff and, in so doing, enhance the individual, faculty and school performance?

Data set 11: Quality learning

Each member of staff was asked to complete a questionnaire with the following questions on 'quality learning':

1. What in your view are the key factors which contribute to 'quality learning'?
2. How do you, as a subject teacher, try to develop skills for quality learning in your lessons?
3. What are the particular strengths of your department in developing quality learning? Can you identify three or more key strategies?

Responses to these questions were the focus for a half-day INSET. Staff discussed their responses in a manner deliberately structured by the ISIS team to ensure that at each point in the debate it was possible to hear what the teacher, teaching team and faculty teams were saying, and to provide inter-faculty discussions to take place. First they reflected on their own and identified on a personal task sheet issues raised by the responses. They then worked in pairs within teaching teams, exchanged their observations and elicited responses. Then they moved into faculty teams and recorded themes and patterns of responses that indicated consensus and areas of difference, and finally they moved into cross-curricular groups, discussed the implications of their conversations and identified areas for action, which were reported back to faculty groups in the form of revised agendas for quality learning. Representatives from each group reported their responses to a whole school staff plenary session.

Data set 12: Outcomes analysed at different 'layers' of the school

In keeping with the concept of the 'layers' of learning it was felt that staff needed to have an opportunity to discuss and investigate the thinking and the practical application that the responses to the questionnaires had raised. A series of

Table 6.7 *Whole School map*

I.T.	Bus. Studies	Health and S.C.	Careers	P.D.	Technology	Science	Maths	Geography	History	R.E.	P.E.	Drama	Music	Art	Library	MFL	English	IDENTIFIED PRIORITIES
					X	X		X									X	Target Setting
					X		X			X	X							Differentiation
					X											X	X	Variety of Learning Activities
					X													Seating Plans
					X								X			X	X	Classroom Management
					X													Create Good Work Atmosphere
					X						X					X	X	Discipline
						X												Clear Introduction to Lesson
						X			X									Make Use of Prior Learning
						X												Open Ended Questioning
						X												Improve Lesson Conclusion
						X												Pupil Purchase of Revision Books
											X							Set High Expectations
											X							Effective Use of Time/Resources
											X							Teacher Knowledge of Activity
								X			X			X			X	Effective Planning
	X									X	X	X	X	X				Use of Assessment
									X	X	X			X				Effective Use of Homework
								X								X		Stimulating Interest
													X			X		Use of Texts/Resources
							X											Use of Praise/Reward
							X											Set Clear Aims and Objectives
									X									Share Ideas with Colleagues
	X																	Develop Independent Learning
	X																	Improve Structure of Course
	X																	Increase Use of Outside Agencies
	X																	Integrate Key Skills
	X																	Greater Use of Extension Work
	X																	Need for Base Room
													X					Consistency of Approach
													X					Plan Deadlines
												X	X					Make Use of Exemplar Work
													X					Emphasis on Key Words
												X	X					Clear Feedback to Pupils
												X						Discussion with Group/Individual
												X						Teacher Exposition
							X											Develop Use of IT
							X											Develop Numeracy Across Curriculum
							X											Develop Effective/Support Team Work

111

discussion meetings were held; some of these involved all staff, some involved the external project consultant, some were small team meetings. In each case the group discussions were collated and distributed to heads of faculties. The outcome of the meetings were given to all teachers and to conclude the activity the faculty groups were asked to reflect on the feedback given and were required to produce a response to the following questions:

1. What are the priorities for your own subject area for development of quality learning in the next twelve months?
2. What are your reasons for selecting these priorities?
3. How do you intend to act on these priorities?

The result was a set of individual subject priorities which, when combined, formed what was called a 'whole school map'. The table indicates all the areas which staff identified as priorities for their quality learning activity.

The deputy headteacher with responsibility for faculty development plans examined the faculty development plans alongside individual subject responses. This had a specific reason: to ensure that the responses arising from the generic faculty were a true reflection of the agenda that all the staff in the faculty had raised. The concern was to ensure that areas of difference were part of the debate and were not avoided or diluted in an effort to avoid contentious issues.

In each of the identified priorities it was clear that there was some overlap amongst themes. It was also clear that within the same school, staff were using different labels to describe the same issue – for example, the English faculty talked about the management of the classroom, and a very similar conversation took place in Technology but was focused on the specifics of the seating plan in class.

Data set 13: The faculty development plans

The collated information from the meetings established a coherent overview of all of the intended developmental activity that teaching staff were intending to undertake in the pursuit of quality learning. This exercise had made transparent what had for all previous years been opaque: staff could look at a simple structured programme of materials and begin to discuss across faculties how they might pair up and support each other as cross-departmental teams in their shared endeavour.

This exercise also allowed all staff to see that there were some areas of work that still needed much more attention.

Two examples of these plans, recorded by the teachers involved, are given here. The bold text indicates the format given to the departments through which responses were analysed.

Art

1. Priorities for quality learning in Art for the next twelve months
- Buy relevant materials
- More stringent planning ahead

- Planning for lessons to add greater diversity
- Review marking and assessing policy
- Review homework policy

2. Reasons for selecting these priorities

There are things going on in Art which work well and I wish to continue these: structure of lessons; displaying work; pupils' expectations generally high; seating plans; classroom management; differentiation; praise, etc.; extracurricular work.

(*a*) Effective use of materials

We generally run out of felts and coloured pencils very quickly. These are used a great deal in the lesson and progress is very often stopped through lack of materials, or the work is not as good as it could be because of inadequate materials.

(*b*) More stringent planning ahead

The curriculum tends not to follow the same projects twice and so planning ahead is not done (I would iike to do a whole year at a time). Because we are always working to new ideas and deadlines (e.g. work to be ready for Arts Festival) it is very difficult to see ahead.

(*c*) Planning for greater diversity

Pupils this year in Years 7–9 have achieved well in completing short pieces of work. They have done well in experimenting with paint. I would also like to spend longer on projects – planning ideas with the pupils, which is required in KS4.

(*d*) Marking and assessment

Whilst there is a policy in place, and it works extremely well, I find it impossible to keep up with *all* the marking.

(*e*) Homework policy

I find homework a problem as it is generally badly done and I spend a long time marking it. I spend a lot of time checking homework in the lessons, reducing time for practical work. Could we think about other forms of available out-of-school study time?

3. How I intend to act on these priorities

I would like to suggest to all school years that they purchase a resource pack so that they can all have their own equipment. I have priced the pack, which would work out at the same price as the sketch pads currently being used.

Another idea for point (*c*) would be to purchase from my capitation sketch pads (Years 7–9) which are used for planning and experimenting with all years. All the planning that the pupils do could be enclosed in a booklet and they could continue to do this at home (thereby coping with the problems of point (*e*)). Assessment could take place on planning and a final piece. This would make marking easier and we could have an evaluation lesson for Years 7–9. This will be very good practice for later in Years 10–11. The stringent planning ahead would therefore be not as important as work with the pupils, who, with help and advice, have a greater freedom in their learning and experiences.

Mathematics

1. Priorities for quality learning in Mathematics

(*a*) Development of use of IT:

Logo

Graphics Calculators

Databases

Spreadsheets

Appropriate software packages

Success Maker

Multi-media

(*b*) Greater use of differentiation and offer challenge to all:

Use of ability groups

Differentiated resources (especially for least able)

Use of assessment records

Use of seating arrangements

Develop independent thinking

(*c*) Development of numeracy across the curriculum

(*d*) Develop more effective and supportive teamwork:

Experienced staff mentoring others taking a corresponding group (especially Years 10 and 11)

Communicate to others what each member of staff has taught

2. Reasons for selecting these priorities

(*a*) Satisfy the demands of National Curriculum

More effective in developing knowledge skills and understanding of pupils

Potency of experience

Offering differentiation

Better resources developed

(*b*) Better accessibility for pupils and so better progress

Develop pupil support for each other

Develop personal skills for independent learning for now and later, and to develop confidence

(*c*) Concentrated effort in developing basic skills to support learning in other areas which in turn further develops the understanding of maths. Build on what will be/is being developed in primary schools

(*d*) Share successes/failures and knowledge/expertise

Share resources and so save time

Teach common topics to parallel groups

Collaborative planning can improve quality of end product and can save time

3. How I intend to act on these priorities

(*a*) INSET

Written into scheme of work

Timetabled use of IT room and written programmes of work

(*b*) Use of assessment information

Development of pupil records

Evaluate published schemes

Consider different working groups and methodologies

More investigations

More progression. Request SEN support

(c) Learn from National Numeracy Project

Collaborations with other subjects

Greater emphasis on oral and mental work

(d) Formal meetings during faculty meeting

Weekly notice board

More learning-focused meetings

Data set 14: Whole school issues

As well as a complete set of faculty development plans, the school was in a position to be able to identify a set of 'whole school issues' from the 'map'. These were drawn from areas where there were known difficulties and disagreements, and from the information gathered during the interviews and questionnaire with Year 9 and Year 10 students:

- Target setting
- Differentiation
- Use of assessment
- Effective use of homework
- How to stimulate pupil interest

Finally, in this phase, the staff came together in an evening staff meeting to focus once more on the whole school map and to see if there were significant themes emerging. Their observations concluded that there were three:

- **Creating the environment for quality teaching and learning** – 'what we do to influence the context within which the teaching and learning takes place'
- **Enhancing the methods for quality teaching and learning** – 'what we do in practical/technical terms to ensure quality in our teaching and learning'
- **Enhancing the structure for quality teaching and learning** – 'what we do to ensure that each teacher and learner has a way of working successfully'

These themes were elaborated by the staff through the use of the whole school map to show what each theme might focus on. Although the themes were not exhaustive they indicated pathways that the teaching and learning agenda had identified, through which a wide range of possible lines of development could be followed (Table 6.8).

Some of these pathways illustrate how this school deepened its own learning through a data-rich investigation into its own workings.

Key issues:

- A redefined series of objectives were established following review

- The focus was now on teaching and learning

- Success was to be established as a result of different layers of impact of the work

---

- New techniques were developed to ensure that teachers' voices were heard

- Difference was looked for and monitored, not as a weakness but as an area in need of further attention

- Activity of different faculties and teaching teams was made transparent

- Cross-curricular teams were encouraged to initiate ideas and innovate

- Whole school objectives were identified as a result of the school data

- New questions emerged in the form of environment, methods and structures for quality learning

Data set 15: Identification of new/shared/tried methodologies

A further area of current interest concerns an area of difference amongst staff. During an earlier meeting unease was expressed on how few methods were being identified by teachers to enhance the quality of teaching and learning. As a result, a short (one-hour) staff meeting was held with the project consultant and a simple strategy to identify and disseminate successful teaching approaches was introduced. This involved staff finding three areas where they felt they could confidently identify an area of strength in their teaching and, correspondingly, three areas where they felt they needed more assistance. The process was team-driven from the outset, and was used to promote a collegial approach to the common problem of teaching in the same place but not necessarily learning from each other at all.

The materials drawn from the session were shared across the departments, but the initiative was not followed up. Without any directives from the senior management team, the staff then took the lead and began a series of cross-teaching team experiments, attempting to introduce and trial new ways of teaching in order to respond to the whole school as well as faculty improvement objectives. The strategies recorded here are just some of the ways that staff had been introducing and sharing their successful approaches. It highlights the differentiated nature of response to the teaching and learning challenge the school had set itself.

What the listing of strategies had allowed staff to do was to explore which teaching approach seemed to work best where. However, the staff wanted to gather evidence to substantiate their feelings. They recognized that there was going to be a limit to this activity within school, and have recently initiated a two-year link with another secondary school from the independent sector to explore and share in a different organizational way.

Table 6.8 *Possible lines of development*

THEME ONE Creating the environment for quality teaching and learning	THEME TWO Enhancing the methods for quality teaching and learning	THEME THREE Enhancing the structure for quality teaching and learning
Seating plans	Variety of activity	Target setting
Management of the classroom	Develop teacher knowledge of the range of activities that can assist boys/girls	Plan effectively for differentiation
Positive working atmosphere	Investigate what interests pupils	Clear introductions to lessons/Improve lesson conclusion
Use of revision books	Use a range of texts	Make use of prior learning
Set high expectations across school	Praise and reward	Open-ended questions
Discipline	Identify and integrate key learning skills	Establish clear aims and objectives
Encourage independent learning	Use exemplar work	Use time effectively
Increase the use of outside agencies	Emphasis on key words	Use assessment in formative and summative ways
Create a resource base room	Give clear feedback to pupils	Use homework in more strategic ways to assist learning
Cross-school use of ICT	Discuss with groups and individuals	Share ideas with colleagues
Cross-school use of numeracy and literacy	Demonstrate to whole class	Develop the structure of the course
Cross-school team work		Extension work Introduce methods to ensure consistency of approach Plan deadlines

Table 6.9 *Methodologies and strategies identified by teachers*

Method	Subject
Whole class teaching	art d&t hum maths pe re eng
Range/individual/pairs, groups	art d&t sci maths eng mfl re pe
Consolidation recap/recall	art d&t hum maths sci mfl eng
Move in/move around class	art dst en
Individual time with teacher	art eng hum
Key skills. words, concepts	hum mfl maths sci
Key question – introductions to the lesson	hum sci maths
Dictation	sci
Summarize key points	hum sci maths eng
Positive marking	sci maths
Timed tasks	sci mfl
Independent learning packages	maths
Problem solving	maths pe
Learning homeworks based around problems	sci
Investigations	maths
Relevance to real world	maths sci
Repetition	eng mfl
Practical followed by discussion	art d&t hum sci
Sharing pupils' work	eng art d&t
Select positive responses	sci s.n. maths mfl eng
Multi-sensory approach	s.n.
Demonstration	art d&t sci pe
Introductions – state aims & objectives	hum eng mfl
Brainstorming	hum eng
Diagrams	hum
Pupil presentation	sci eng art
Differentiated tasks	maths hum
Video	hum

Table 6.9 *continued*

Mobile phone	mfl
Music	mfl
'Hot-seating'	eng
Model answers	eng
'Going for 5'	eng
Review of rewards/sanctions	maths sen sci
Games	mfl
Audio aids	mfl
Visual aids	mfl
Overhead transparencies	sci mfl
Humour	sci
Role-play	sci hum
Structured speaking and listening	sci eng
Art	eng mfl hum

art = art   d&t = design & technology   hum = humanities   re = religion
eng = English   maths = mathematics   mfl = modern foreign languages
pe = physical education   sen = special educational needs

COMMENTARY: LEARNING TO LIVE WITH COMPLEXITY – AN EMERGING LEARNING SCHOOL

This case study reports a school undergoing a process of learning, starting from some initial steps where it began thinking about a quite focused set of initiatives designed to inform how to improve boys' performance, going through a period of modification of approach to begin to include the student voice, and leading to a redesign of the whole improvement approach that they took to ensure that their primary focus was on learning and that all other aspects of school development led towards the enhanced ability of staff and students to learn.

During this period staff underwent the emotional highs and lows of team development, establishing new working relationships across and within teams, having to take difficult decisions about the implications of change agendas that they faced, and have slowly moved into an organizational culture which is more experimental, more willing to take risks in its managerial approach to ensure that staff can gather what they feel are the necessary supporting strategies to allow them to learn from each other in the pursuit of quality learning.

It is worth remembering from the outset of this discussion that the process of change being described here was dynamic and evolving. The staff maintained their energy through a combination of areas of common agreement and areas of challenge and difference. There were times when the activity that took place was underdeveloped, raw and unfocused; there were other times when it was deliberate and purposeful. The subsequent conversations held between teachers, students and more recently in parental consultations have, in turn, facilitated predictable and unpredictable responses from staff, which have then been developed into organizational activity. These activities created tensions which could be seen in the varying opinions of staff, students and parents to changes and to data presented. Some of the findings reinforced ways of thinking, working and seeing school; other findings, however, challenged those conceptualizations and raised new and different ways of considering the problem of how to improve the learning taking place, demanding a more integrated and systemic viewpoint from the whole staff. The extent to which the school, as a community, came to terms with the challenge of these new possibilities is, for me, the indication that the school was evolving into a different type of organizational configuration, evolving into a learning school.

To make sense of the process of learning that the school went through, I have shaped the story of the changes and the debates taking place around them in different phases of growth (see Clarke, 1998 for a more detailed discussion of this method). These phases capture characteristic patterns of activity which reflect the thinking, the ways that school was working, the direction in which it saw the changes tending. When combined, these phases provide an insight into what the school felt it was important to establish in the form of outcome and what these collected themes represented in terms of an underlying set of assumptions about the organizational structure that was being worked with in order to make the desired change occur.

The developmental pattern of the school can be summarized as follows:

Seeking certainty
Externally referenced to OFSTED key issues
Internal hierarchy
Core team established
Each team member had responsibilities
Data gathered and analysed
Data reported to staff

Identifying new possibilities
Outside consultation
Student voice listened to
The emergence of an internal configuration of response
Cross-team activity
Staff listening to each other on areas of concern
Developing a collective consensus of the characteristics of under-performance

Complex formulations
Systemic activities
Playing a role as formulators of approaches to inform strategy
Looking beyond the previous organizational structure to gain new insights into their organizational reality
Continued outreach

Linking to the network
Increasing links with other schools
Using parental ideas and developmental opinions
Using student voice

Steering a new course
Redefining the developmental agenda to suit learning needs

From this overview of the pattern of reform we are able to identify four phases of growth. The four phases described in this school's learning journey's were:

- Phase 1: Seeking certainty;
- Phase 2: Identifying new possibilities;
- Phase 3: Complex formulations;
- Phase 4: Steering a new course.

Phase 1: Seeking certainty

When I began working with this school, it was focused on the use of the external OFSTED inspection as its primary means of identification of improvement areas. The key areas for action had specified the need to tackle the matter of significant under-performance of boys in school.

The inspection report prompted developmental approaches in the school which could be placed within the modern conceptualization of improvement. The strategic decision-making process was dominated by the thinking of the senior management team, who were in turn 'led' by the definition of 'their' school problems by an external source of power and authority.

Having selected a strategic approach, the hierarchical structure of the school set in motion a series of predictable strategic responses to the identified problem. Running parallel to this series of data-collecting activities, a predictable organizational method was initiated to undertake the tasks that the improvement theme had identified. This behaviour can be characterized as ritualistic improvement. It represented an organizational method with which the school was familiar and which was uncontested and accepted as the way things got done. It required particular members of staff to play out their role within an uncontested hierarchical arrangement. The acceptance of external pointers for development by school senior staff, the strategic plan for response that they established and the creation of a core team charged with the job of improving boys' performance bear witness to the formula of the ritual being played through.

Each core team member then drew upon her professional experience and defined the problem through readily available data sets which to a great extent served to confirm what staff, and therefore school, already knew. This form of data-led inquiry was thus both a 'safe' and a predictable procedure, bearing all the hallmarks of closed change. Such a procedure is not contested, it is dealing with information about which the staff already have shared opinions,, and it does nothing to challenge the organizational approach. In this case, it provided senior management with answers to their inquiry in the form of concrete details on matters such as attendance, detentions, and differences in performance in particular subject areas.

This form of data-led inquiry also provided opportunities for disagreement in interpretation of what the data meant, but because of the type of data acquired this disagreement was of little real consequence, because it was framed inside the existing power relationships in the hierarchy. Whilst disagreement and difference were valued and acknowledged within the organizational climate, they had no particular impact because, although staff points of view might be sought at the personal level, staff knew, just as senior management knew, that positions would not be changed as a result of differences, because the organizational way of working was to fit into the hierarchy and to stick to the approaches that experience told them would provide the answers. In this case, the locus of attention was therefore on what was 'wrong' with the students (particularly boys), and how, once the problem had been identified, it could then be solved.

When it became necessary for these data to be shared with all staff in the form of consultation, the members of the core team identified indicators arising from the data prior to the staff meeting, rather than using the meeting to generate the indicators from the grass roots. This had the effect of 'informing' staff of findings, rather than consulting and seeking advice.

The ritualized sequence of the modern paradigm was therefore completed. School played out an illusion of improvement through the acceptance that the generalized findings on boys' under-performance would solve the problem, through the role-conscious hierarchical management of the working group and through the types of data that were examined and interpreted. The message was clear that the role of the staff, just like that of the students, was to do what they were told – a reflection of the socio-political environment in which the school was itself operating, being told what to improve by external 'others'.

We witness, in this first phase, two important 'improvement' process indicators being drawn upon: ritual and experience. However, on their own, these serve to close down, rather than broaden, possibilities for change. Assumed rituals and experience inside a modern environment serve an underlying structure that allows secure, certain and formulaic approaches to improvement to be adopted. These are managerially and technically carried through by willing participants who draw upon their own experience of working within this type of organizational culture to reinforce the particular paradigmatic view.

Phase 2: Identifying new possibilities

A much harder question to work out is what prompted this staff and school to begin to change their way of operating. I think that there are two factors of considerable significance.

First was the arrival of a different voice. In the case of this school, this was the direct involvement of the external consultant and, more significantly for the challenge to ways of seeing the school, the arrival of a student voice in the data collection process. The raising of different voices meant having to 'hear' a view of the school from a different perspective. Unlike OFSTED, neither voice held any power, so they represented no threat to the established order. But they did think, work and see the improvement issue from competing and therefore different perspectives.

Second, and directly associated to this matter of different perspectives, was the political decision by management to listen to these different voices. This deliberate action directed their activity towards the interface between the modern and beyond-modern way of living and working in the schools. It shook the interpersonal fabric of the school and caused members of the school community to begin to identify possibilities from which to inform and develop their work.

The use of the interviews with students and the questionnaires opened up a set of new investigative features to the school. It challenged the certainty of viewpoint of both senior management, the core team and, significantly, the teaching staff. It did this because it brought these different players into the organizational conversations and changed how the staff saw the configuration of the problem that they faced. In particular, it began a process of 'tuning-in', where staff began to hear what students were saying, to think about the problems that they were raising from their perspective and, in so doing, to see the role that they had in inhibiting or enhancing student performance. This in turn, gave staff a sense of utility: they could participate and have an effect through their role in making a difference in each faculty, in classrooms through their teaching, and in their response to the stated learning needs of the students. There was a different orientation in the investigations, from areas of certainty – what staff already knew and needed to have confirmed – to areas which they could use to inform where they moved to next. This was evident in the willingness to use open-ended interview material as a catalyst for investigation into what students felt were areas of concern and potential improvement.

As staff became more involved in tuning-in and hearing what other people were saying about school, they returned to some of the earlier 'ritualized' data sets, but pursuing slightly different interests. The conversations between staff changed from solely departmental to more inter-departmental discussions, sharing with each other information on what they were doing and whether it seemed to be working. The use of the data began to stimulate activity lower down in school, where smaller teams came together to explore more closely the teaching and learning interface. Interaction increased in frequency and was moving from directed to more self-regulatory, more investigative inquiry for personal and team benefits, on things that staff felt they could change.

Tuning-in to hearing other people's voices on the improvement agenda also raised some specific questions with staff. They began to identity a differentiated pattern of performance in different subjects, and this prompted further debate on how to proceed and how to intervene.

This second phase illustrated two further improvement processes at work, both of which served to indicate the importance of sustained conversation. These were attunement and interaction. These combined with the organizational ritual and personal experience of staff and began to form a quite different organizational configuration in the school.

Phase 3: Complex formulations

The orientation of the initiative began to turn slowly towards a deeper investigation into school learning about its own provision for learning. The work had begun to generate a dynamic of its own, where staff were more willing to participate and introduce ideas. However, there was still an underlying structure that bore out modern viewpoints. Tensions were evident between staff wanting to push forward with new ways of working with students and between departments and other staff who were less forthcoming.

The core team undertook a review of what had been learnt and concluded that some concerns were emerging from staff about where the work might go next. The process had generated a vast data set and had spawned meetings and discussion groups and what began to emerge was an underlying tension: should this be tied down at this point, or do we allow it to continue to run?

This represented, to me, evidence of activity at the interface between the paradigms – the beyond-modern transition point. As I said at the start of this section, this is a dynamic process, it ebbs and flows. As one set of expectations about approaches to the work, the ideas and the structures ascends and begins to become more commonplace, the declining approaches of the previous order occasionally rise up again and create tensions.

During this period a noticeable stabilizing feature was activity that centred around teaching. The development of the 'characteristics of under-performance' materials, and the types of interventions that staff used in response, brought a material focus on the conversations. Those staff who sought solace in the modern view felt that they had something tangible from the initiative that they could use, and other staff who were interested in how to begin to alter the ways staff looked at their role as teachers were content because they felt that the conversations were getting to the 'core of the matter'.

The improvement messages drawn from this stage are concerned with this complexity. The principal activity was clearly moving the staff towards a focus on learning, and to create the climate for this to happen inside it was necessary to develop strategic thinking in as many teaching staff as possible so that they could play a part in the development and become formulators of activity rather than implementors. This began to be demonstrated through the emphasis on cross-faculty developments, and was amplified in the fourth and final phase.

Phase 4: Steering a new course

As the case history indicates, Phase 4 began with a period of stocktaking. Senior management drew in what had been learnt and, working in collaboration with staff, reconstructed the focus into a series of objectives so that it was legitimized inside the structures required of the school in the wider environment in which it operated. The focus was now on teaching and learning, where success was to be established as a result of different layers of impact of the work taking place, at whole school, teams, and classroom levels.

By this phase the school was tentatively steering a new course using what they called the Quality Learning Initiative as the pathmaker for improvement activity. Features of this work were the attempts being made to lead the school into being able to manage diversity and difference. To facilitate this, and to move it to a point of ritual (thus replacing the old order with the new), new techniques were developed to ensure that teacher, student and, more recently, parental voice was heard.

Learning leadership features as a theme cutting across almost all school agendas for development. Senior management, along with faculty heads, tried to ensure that difference was looked for and monitored, not as a weakness but as an area in need of further attention. For some middle managers this was a difficult personal matter, and school sometimes demonstrated the precarious nature of the changes taking place by resorting to old rituals of 'rank pulling' to force compliance. Despite these frequent setbacks, as some of the evidence from the fourth phase shows, the degree of cross-school transparency of strategy and discussion changed as a result of the leadership efforts being made by all staff to improve learning and teaching.

The school has now come to a threshold point. It is slowly getting better at living with complexity. As its experience of the new approaches develops and it begins to interact and learn how to develop in ways that serve its own organizational needs, its ability to tune in and identify intervention points will move. The critical component, which I believe is missing now in the development of this school towards one that can consolidate at the modern paradigm and sustain that activity, is how it begins to learn to facilitate new links into the wider community. This part of the story remains to be told.

In the third part of this book I will discuss how schools might be guided to certain types of questions which in turn can point them towards different pathways for improvement.

KEY ISSUES AND IDEAS IN THIS CHAPTER

- The case study describes a school evolving through a process of first external and then internal inquiry.
- This process was a dynamic flow of response to and action from the identification of issues.
- Some of the approaches the school took reinforced their previous ideas, others initiated new change agendas.
- Four learning phases were described:
  - Seeking certainty
  - Identifying new possibilities
  - Complex formulations
  - Steering a new course
- These phases capture different 'improvement' characteristics:
  - Ritual
  - Experience
  - Attunement
  - Intervention

- Management
- Learning leadership
- I suggest that these characteristics serve as features along a transitional trajectory from modern to beyond-modern schools. As schools begin to learn, they draw upon resources that these labels capture to either consolidate what they are already doing, or to push forward their learning
- Finally, in this case study we can see some examples of how a school moves over a period of time. I chose deliberately not to make the time link evident because I believe that this interferes with the central message I am trying to make that the critical matter here concerns a search for what the person, and in the is case the school determines to be 'truth'. This means that it is the process of thinking that matters. As it is the choices that lead from the thinking that liberate or inhibit schools. Some schools take a lot longer to find this than others.

Part 3: Seeing the Journey

Learn as much as you can, to become as much as you can, so as to give as much as you can.
Thomas Aquinas

In the first part of this book I argued that we need to reconceptualize the purpose of schools to suit an emerging world view. This world view is represented in a paradigm shift that draws upon political, economic, ecological, social, spiritual, technological and scientific thinking and fuses them into an integrative rather than individualistic conceptual view. In so doing, I suggested that we need to correspondingly rethink change so that its approach better suits our times. To assist this thinking I presented a conceptual interpretation of paradigms of change in the form of a growth map. This instrument allows us to examine the 'mindset' of the school theoretically in order to begin to establish a profile of the organization. Through the second part of the book I have shown how some of the activity of the school, if seen through the lens of this re-conceptualization, begins to make a new type of sense. It represents a new normalization process based around a 'local' to 'global' interpretation of the system, where schools operate inside broader learning networks. This development represents a re-norming – a transitional process of evolution where the culture of the school shifts from one way of doing things to another. As the activity of the new way of working increases, so too does the redesign of other aspects of the system to better suit our new understanding of need.

In this third and final part I want to turn my attention to the matter of how we might facilitate this improvement process so that it becomes an established system. I want to suggest that we have to grasp a basic concept: that schools are at the same time both singular and collective units of growth functioning inside a network, and whatever is happening at the level of the school is going to have an impact elsewhere as a result of the interconnections, be they deliberate or serendipitous.

So, if we accept that every school represents a unique configuration of people, experience, location and potential, despite the uniqueness of the school configuration, we will also observe that patterns of activity emerge from single school configurations that are of value to other organizational sites and influence the systemic response to the context inside which they function.

In Chapter 1 I raised the direction which my search is taking when I gave a case for the creation of networks. The network can either be a deliberately established system or it can happen by default. If it becomes part of a deliberate and consciously designed system, it will be developed through thinking that leads towards a synthesis of successful approaches to teaching and learning, it will function in a non-linear way and it will capture the essence of the ecological paradigm representing values of co-operation, partnership and conservation of success in the pursuit of quality learning. If it happens by default, it will remain under-conceptualized, and when links between schools do emerge they will operate on a more linear basis and will have to struggle to overcome a competitive orientation.

While a system remains in transition the concept of school and network raises a series of challenges: in particular, the development of ways of 'seeing' improvement as both school and network active, the 'systemic' viewpoint which can observe detail and dynamics at play. Our challenge lies in how to live with this complexity, and how we learn to see and respond to the range of challenges it will raise.

As I described in Chapter 4, each configuration of school will emphasize dominant paradigmatic preferences for the improvement process, and this enables us to make distinctions between them. These differences facilitate discussion about the type of supporting architecture – the structures and methods – we might best promote at an individual or school level inside the dominant paradigm of modernism or, in addition, at an intra-school level if we are to establish a community of 'learning schools' in the ecological paradigm. Attention to these differences will allow us to identify and articulate the 'expression' and 'achievement' (Olds, 1992) of the new paradigm.

I have suggested that the configuration heightens the possibility for discussions to begin which can focus on intervention processes, and which will lead to optimization techniques for the modern and beyond-modern transition. These can be described (indeed, the canon of improvement literature does so in the case of the modern, and increasingly indicates what we might 'do' in our transition to the beyond-modern). I have tried to extend these descriptions in this book by making clear distinctions between the type of thinking about schools and the thinking about learning raised by the modern paradigm and the transition to the beyond-modern. In the case of the ecological paradigm, I think we can sketch out some of the territory that the learner and school might explore if they were to operate there (the discussion on the ISIS initiative is an example), but we have not as yet got there.

So, to proceed, I want to focus my attention in this final part of the book on the development of a complex learning system (Fullan, 1999) within the emerging 'ecological' paradigm. I will do this by raising some questions and challenges that we might need to consider and respond to as we take steps from one phase of our learning to another.

Chapter 7

Daring to Tell the Stories of the Future

I would like to leave behind me the conviction that if we maintain a
certain amount of caution and organisation we deserve victory . . .
You cannot carry out fundamental change without a certain
amount of madness. In this case, it comes from non-conformity, the
courage to turn your back on the old formulas, the courage to invent
the future. It took the madmen of yesterday for us to be able to act
with extreme clarity today. I want to be one of those madmen. We
must dare to invent the future.
      Thomas Sankara, Speech at the Congress of African States

I have argued that schools face a turbulent and paradoxical moment in their evolution as they come to terms with changing demands of their meaning and purpose in contemporary society. On their own the teacher, the team, the whole school might feel overwhelmed in the face of their perception of the wider turmoil of competing systems. However, I believe that schools who begin to experiment with new ways of defining the learning agenda and giving students greater say in the process are already daring to talk and to tell the stories of a different future; they have turned a corner and are embarking on a quite different journey from that which they previously undertook.

As they proceed they will have to face choices. These are both personal and collective challenges. They will have to come to terms with the fact that to begin to embrace a 'learning-centred' school they will need to deal consciously with the complexity of what it is to function and live inside a less than certain organizational environment, where there will have to be a changed mantra from the 'defined' and 'determined' to the 'flexible' and 'evolving'. For many years schools have been operating on the assumption of underlying structures of stability, harmony, consensus and steady growth (Clarke, forthcoming). Indeed, these conditions have often been presented to schools as optimal states from which to develop (DfEE, 1997a, p. 205). A paradigm shift places these conditions under scrutiny, as they no longer represent the most realistic interpretation of the school environment which is being developed. Indeed, I suggest that they represent a view of reality of schools which is now misleading and inappropriate, failing to capture the dynamics at play in a network system.

Given an interpretation of schools functioning in a climate of disorder and critical tension, with no clear plan for them to adhere to about the appropriacy of the next steps they should take but a connection of units operating within and between schools, all focused on the objective of enhancing learning, we can ask: How and on what should schools concentrate their efforts in order to demonstrate to themselves that they are still seeking truth on difficult, uncharted ground?

In response to this question I want to point towards what schools might examine inside and between their organizations. As they consider what to look at they can begin to think about how they might respond. The material comes from the work that I have undertaken with schools in single case studies, and inside the network activity of the Improving Standards In Schools (Tameside LEA) and Celebrating and Extending Achievement initiatives (Bury LEA 1995 to the present time).

What should schools look towards as they move into the ecological paradigm?

- **A redefinition of control** – How might 'control' be reconsidered inside the school system at national, regional, school and classroom levels? The new understanding of control raises the importance of 'implementers becoming formulators' (Mintzberg, 1994) so that learners have more control over their own learning, and managers relinquish it and offer greater opportunities for teachers to take control of their own work.
- **The appropriate uses of power** – By whom, on whom, for whose benefit? This challenge asks whom schools are for and how the present structures within and between schools support inappropriate forms of organizational power that 'teach' students irrelevant and dated ways of seeing organizations at work.
- **The self-organizing of learning teams** – How can activity that is geared towards school improvement be more fluid, more empowering and use the capacity of all learners to best effect within and between schools? This challenge anticipates alternative ways of seeing learning, as emergent rather than predefined opportunities for growth.
- **An appreciation of multiplicity of view** – This challenge recognizes the importance of difference within and between schools by asking how we can ensure new perspectives and diverse ideas are accommodated into the fabric of the improvement approaches that the school and the network take.
- **A willingness to take risks** – This challenge concerns the unknown. How does the system respond to risk? What constitutes risk in school and the network? Why do we see it as risk? How can risk be developed as a strategic activity to enable all agents in the system to benefit as learners?
- **Learning to learn in groups** – How do we promote review time and feedback sessions, how do we maintain discussions over long time frames and identify the patterns of success and failure, how do we avoid learning barriers?
- **A need to create space** – This challenge involves the creation of time to allow differences that have been identified to be examined and debated. It requires choices to be made and justified by asking 'What can we lose from our present working activity so that other time is created to do more important things?'

A REDEFINITION OF CONTROL

The Dance of the Fossils (Baudrillard, 1994) illustrated graphically the criticism of a preoccupation with modern methods of management, designed as they are on controlling those 'lower down' in the hierarchy. Most noticeably, government continues to adopt such approaches through crude, domineering techniques intent on telling school communities how they can manage improvement in teaching and learning. Even when the policy is polished to provide an illusion of compliance and partnership the control and power remain central. Whilst there will be little real enhancement of the underlying thinking and approach at the government level of activity, for politicians are invariably last to see the changes on the ground (Capra, 1996), considerable changes are taking place in the workplace which indicate a new understanding of the meaning of control (Binney and Williams, 1995).

The case study in Chapter 6 illustrated a transition that came about because teachers wanted to understand more about what they did in classrooms with learners. The only way for them to gather the relevant data to inform their work was to make a transition from being implementors to formulators. They moved from being told what to look for by outsiders to looking for what they felt their school needed to address. They took control of their own improvement agenda. As a result they gained considerably more control over the pace, manner and direction of the improvement initiative and its focus on learning and teaching. Once this territory had been covered improvement would never be the same again.

> *It was like we had crossed the threshold, it created a buzz that I haven't encountered here before.*
> *(Teacher of Mathematics, school case study)*

Although at this stage the redesign of the control inside the case study school is perhaps more symbolic than real, in that it has yet to prove to be a sustained process because the school is struggling with the internal turmoil of being on the interface of two paradigms at managerial and personal levels, it has demonstrable effects as the students' voice was heard, their ideas were used strategically, and new features of the improvement agenda were raised as a result.

I have noticed that 'control' of conversations changes as schools begin to think about what and how they are learning. In the early stages of the school developments in the network, each school was careful to ensure that they could explain every minute aspect of their activity as a series of events each of which was justified; they had in a sense to hold on to all of the arguments. This led to extremely long meetings, where each detail of the activity of the school was reported. As the schools became more interested in what was changing, how attitudes were shifting, how staff and students were working together to focus more on the shared interest in learning, the focus of the conversation shifted from attention on immediate responses to identified problems, reflecting a need to hold on to all the activity, to a wider, more fluid and sometimes intuitive consideration of what might be influencing the problem and what series of approaches when brought together, could form a more sustained response. Their 'control' orientation was no longer linear, it was non-linear and interested in connecting and contextualizing emerging understanding.

Control can be understood in similar ways in the network, where the collective energy of the team, confident in their shared experience, often provided opportunities to step outside the restrictions of many of the more formal meeting styles and empowered them with the added dimension of strategic approaches and ideas no longer remaining context-bound within a single school view. This freedom enabled conversations to take place that probably would not have done so inside school, within the security of the network team. It provided an opportunity for staff to explore and experiment with ideas outside of the normal school-controlled areas, where people were less inclined to cling onto 'their' ideas and were more willing to listen to a range of alternatives.

The focus of control in the ecological paradigm should be on approaches that are sustainable, repeatable and of collective value. These are undefined, and deliberately remain so at this point. To achieve a redefinition of control is to abandon a view of school improvement that assumes it is possible to journey along a predetermined route by ticking off the milestones of a plan, in favour of a new type of control which develops the skill of 'seeing' the complexity of the school community and the supporting network. To identify sustainable, repeatable practice means to ask the following types of question across the school community:

- Who establishes the controls in your school in the areas of teaching, learning, organization of school and curriculum?
- Who controls the processes of learning in your school in these four domains?
- Who should decide on learning style, on teaching style?
- How do learners exercise control of their learning in school?
- Do learners have any influence on teaching, learning, organization or curriculum?
- If so, where and why?
- Does this represent a transformational approach, or does it reinforce the existing patterns of working?
- If you pursue further the answers you have gathered, what do you see as the major advantages ands disadvantages you will encounter?
- Would you be willing to go further with the agendas for change that you and your school raise?

Redefining control by giving it to those who have little or none establishes organizational journeys which encourage commitment, involvement and a sense of 'participation in creating something better', as staff and students begin to frame and model their views of school reality and of how they can begin to redefine and challenge some of those given realities that inhibit learning. It represents a significant challenge to the modern paradigm.

THE APPROPRIATE USES OF POWER

The questions of what the school does in its role as educator and the methods it selects to undertake its activity are closely related to the issue of power. If we revisit one of the 'learning themes' that I raised in Chapter 1 (Table 1.1) we recognize that school could be a place where power is made transparent as part of a political dimension of learning about democratic processes. In most cases schools exercise power unquestioningly, 'on' staff as well as students and parents. In doing so, their appropriateness of use is frequently for organizational rather than student benefit.

In reality most schools assume power over students, and so they inhibit the opportunities for the individuals to learn important lessons about making choices and understanding the consequences of power within a safe environment.

The case study of the school in Chapter 6 illustrated how power can be exercised through both hierarchical and collaborative approaches within the same organization and how, at times, this becomes contested and challenged as well as accepted and worked with. If we are to move towards an integrative ecological paradigm, a more equitable and transparent form of power needs to be developed within the improvement process. This will draw attention to ways in which schools assume power over students and by doing so present new learning opportunities concerned with choice and voice and the role of the individual within a community (Neill, 1992).

It is worth noting that a frequently cited research report (Sammons, Hillman and Mortimore, 1995) recognized 'pupils rights and responsibilities' as one of the eleven key factors of effective schools. This characteristic was then subdivided into three features: raising self-esteem, establishing positions of authority, and control of work. Whilst the first of these is obviously of vital importance for the psychological well-being of the student, the latter two are manifestations of the biased distribution of power that students experience daily within schools. This is a matter that is barely addressed at all in schools. If taken seriously, the redistribution of power could alter the ways in which schools operate and promoting rights and responsibilities could be a democratic feature of a learning school. If students are given responsibility, they gain that without any recourse to power delegated to them from people who have both rights and responsibilities. Serious attention to such issues is a necessary component of the development of the school community into one that trusts all learners and challenges itself to trust the devolution of power to learners to facilitate their learning.

Power is a silent partner in the improvement of schools, it receives little mention and yet it sits there, enabling or inhibiting change. As a daily feature of the life of the improvement work I was involved in, power was experienced through the work inside collaborative teams as they exercised choices and determined courses of action. It was also experienced as the deliberate blocking of change, through the intransigence of senior personnel unwilling to redesign their system so as to accommodate new approaches and through middle management's unwillingness to release their hold on how a department should function. This was evident in the manner in which the network teams shared designs and shaped new strategies together. Their frustrations emerged when they realized that sometimes their status inside school simply did not 'pull any weight'.

The appropriate use of power through teams within networks rather than in the form of hierarchy makes power more transparent as an influential feature in the process of change. Discussion of choices and the reasons for structures and systems can illustrate to learners the forms of organizational behaviour that are relevant and adaptive, or dated and inappropriate. In the transition from a modern to an ecological paradigm the investigation of power across networks and inside schools is a vital part of the architecture of the system. We have to relocate at grass-roots level, to redesign powerful learning that lives up to its name (Joyce, Calhoun and Hopkins, 1997).

Some questions to raise about power in schools and in school improvement might be:

- Whom are schools for?
- How is power exercised in your school?
- Are you in a position to influence decisions?
- Do you participate in or receive improvement agendas?
- How does your school make its power transparent?
- Does this use of power represent a transformational approach, or does it reinforce the existing patterns of working?
- If you pursue further the answers you have gathered, what do you see as the major advantages and disadvantages you will encounter?
- Would you be willing to go further with the agendas for change that you and your school raise?

THE SELF-ORGANIZING OF LEARNING TEAMS

The foregoing discussion on the challenge raised by redistributing power brings me to the next challenge, which concerns the self-organizing of learning teams. To place trust in learners by relinquishing power to them so they can make choices of their own is also to believe that there is a potential for self-organizing in each person, each learning community and each network. This is a political statement, suggesting that learners can manage themselves and that the assistance they require is in focusing on choices concerned with *how* to learn as much as on *what* to learn. Learning how to learn often becomes neglected because of pressure to take examinations and to fit within a system. In the present crisis, where we see a small, permanently excluded 'underclass' (Hart, 1997) grouping of students who will never reach the much-lauded academic requirements of five A–C grades in the GCSE examination at 16+, the issue of how to learn is a missing but vital component for these students, together with the question of what this 'underclass' of learners should perhaps be learning in schools if they are not in a position to become incorporated into the A–C band.

Contrastingly, the self-organizing learner makes a series of choices based on needs and constructs meaningful tasks and approaches to achieve those tasks which, given the appropriate circumstances, can be validly recognized as achievement.

Such self-organization implies a need for space, a need for the opportunity to have assistance and support when necessary, and a need to have access to appropriate resources.

Driven by a concern to explore what type of curriculum might best suit the needs of young learners in preparation for adult life in twenty years' time, an example has been described in the current work being developed by the Royal Society of Arts (see Chapter 2), which is exploring the ideas of a competence-based curriculum. Through this curriculum structure a range of learning modules become possible. These modules can be based around specific life experiences, which will place students in contexts which demand a range of responses concerned with how to manage people, situations, information, being a citizen, and how to learn from such experiences. An example is given in Table 7.1.

Table 7.1 *Modelling a learning system*

Categories	Situations
Competences	Understand how to manage risk and uncertainty, the wide range of contexts in which these will be encountered, and techniques for using them
Rationale	Change is an ordinary feature of our personal and organizational lives
Learning outcomes	Able to meet, share ideas and develop trust in working with a new group of learners
Contexts	Starting a new school
Illustrative material	Building new learning teams Establishing a group ethos
System development	Develop learning team approach Network ideas across the teams for shared strategies

This type of work is within our grasp, but it demands new liberties which promote an understanding of the micro-political implications of the delegation of power and the self-organization of learning communities at a local level, where not all the choices that the school might take will be in line with that which the LEA advocates or the central government intends. Questions that the challenge of self-organizing learning groups raises are:

- What opportunities exist for learners (staff or students) to self-organize?
- How is learning (staff or students) 'managed' on a day-to-day basis?
- What messages does this give to learners (staff or students)?
- How do staff and students learn to learn in school?
- What changes might your school have to make to facilitate a self-organizing dimension to learning?
- Who would be most threatened?
- Does the use of self-organizing learning teams reinforce the existing patterns of working or does it transform previous approaches?

- If you pursue further the answers you have gathered, what do you see as the major advantages and disadvantages you will encounter?
- Would you be willing to go further with the agendas for change that you and your school raise?

AN APPRECIATION OF MULTIPLICITY OF VIEW

The recognition that there are many possible routes to achieving a goal and as many goals as we desire to set is uncomfortable within an individualistic paradigm, because its divergence implies a lack of control.

In the case study, the school-wide investigation into teaching styles raised the issue of difference in a transparent way for all staff to identify and to then consider what they might do with the differences they had identified. The resulting team approaches to sharing successful strategies heightened the teachers' awareness of the power of integrative strategy. The same method of adopting a focus, analysing one's own practice, pairing up with colleagues and sharing insights was a feature of the network activity. It merits considerable attention as a way of transforming the systemic skill base of the profession.

I would like to see the advancement of a new networking foundation which thrives on the recognition of this need and the duty of the school to seek out the ways in which each learner is best suited to learn. The 'basics', in such a system, would be diverted away from a sterile debate on the content issues of what to teach and how to teach maths and language, towards a comprehensive understanding of what to teach particular learners according to how they seem most suited to learn. The teacher is therefore engaged in the career-long pursuit of understanding the nature of teaching and facilitating for a diversity of learning needs. Similarly, there should be a renewal of the ways of looking at supporting teaching staff in their own learning, so that their learning hopes are explored fully and serious commitment is made to those hopes being realized within the teaching career. Relevant questions are:

- Who is listened to in your school?
- Are they influential as a result?
- How does school accommodate the views of other agencies into its developmental agenda?
- Does school listen to and take seriously the voice of students?
- How does the student voice get heard?
- How does the 'dissenting' voice get heard in school, or does it?
- What defence mechanisms does the school use to prevent certain people or organizations from being heard?
- Does the use of different opinions reinforce the existing patterns of working or does it transform previous approaches?
- If you pursue further the answers you have gathered, what do you see as the major advantages and disadvantages you will encounter?
- Would you be willing to go further with the agendas for change that you and your school raise?

A WILLINGNESS TO TAKE RISKS

Our school system does not like risk, although, paradoxically, it is at the very heart of learning. Educating for risk involves thinking creatively, making a challenge to the conventional patterns of thinking and seeking patterns that promote new possibilities. The schools that show exceptional results and rounded learners are often those schools that approach the conventional with an unconventional perspective.

Risk is one of the undiscussable aspects of improvement because it inevitably implies unknown territory to be crossed, with no plan and no idea of where the journey might lead. When we learn we cherish the tangible quality of our work and we push forward the ideas on many fronts without necessarily being certain of the implications of our actions. We are challenged to take risks if we want to change how we do things, and we can make this risk-taking easier. In the example of the network, the collective desire to generate knowledge initiated school activity which used the larger community to legitimize riskier activity in the pursuit of new ideas. In the school case study, what the staff did in relocating a debate about the improvement of boys' performance to the student level was, in retrospect – though not in foresight – a risky venture. Staff spoke after the interview material had been presented about the initiative being a 'brave move'; just as when crossing danger-ous ravines, it is often the view from the other side that puts the risk into perspective.

It is a vital feature of a learning school that it will take risks in order to survive. Risk implies conflict, disagreement, disorder, and an amplification at times of inconsistent actions amongst staff. The alternative is not to take risks, to apply overarching consistencies through applied vision and values and plans. This is no longer an option, as no single person or school can possibly have the depth of knowledge or the breadth of skill to deal with all that change will throw at it. Modern viewpoints ultimately block organizational learning, because all evidence that emerges to the contrary view of the hierarchy is rejected.

When a state takes the perspective that it knows what is right, the school will inevitably find its internal perspectives being rejected in favour of the more powerful external view, and the inconsistencies emerge. This makes risk-taking approaches important, as it creates an internal dynamic for potential growth (Fullan, 1999). We attempt to alter the mindset to acknowledge that there is no solution to the problem being experienced, but that there are better ways of thinking, ways that enable people to live with the complexity of the learning that tells us we can exist in such states of risk permanently.

The following are some questions raised by a consideration of risk and risk-taking:

- What constitutes risk in your school?
- Are some forms of information too challenging to deal with at present?
- If so, what is stopping you from dealing with them?
- Do you have strategies for taking risks?
- Are you able to recognize the pattern of activity that is leading staff to want to move into uncharted ground?

whose support could you usefully draw upon to make the nature of the risk
more transparent?

Does the use of different opinion reinforce the existing patterns of working or
does it transform previous approaches?

- If you pursue further the answers you have gathered, what do you see as the
major advantages and disadvantages you will encounter?
- Would you be willing to go further with the agendas for change that you and
your school raise?

LEARNING TO LEARN IN GROUPS

If teams begin to work in more complex ways trying to link together series of data
sets drawing upon diverse opinions so as to broaden the scenarios open to them,
they will discover other ways of thinking about problems and of learning about
responses. Their learning will open up the possibility that others think differently
about the same issue, and that they too believe in their approach. This was a
feature of both the school case study and the network example. As a result of
identifying similarity and difference people will choose either to move position,
influenced by the counter-argument, or to initiate challenges to the others' reality.
To do this successfully, and to use the outcomes of the new learning fully, we need
to create situations where teams seek their own ways of working closely
together.

The case study showed how the deliberate process of moving from the whole
school, to team, to cross-school teams, to links within the network sustained a
variety of conversations on areas of work that mattered to the people involved.
These are not likely to arise from pre-packaged courses, because these are often
designed without the team agenda in mind. It is appropriate to raise here the
school improvement maxim of 'sustained effort'. The efforts will have to address
team viewpoints, personal viewpoints and school viewpoints, and the agendas will
reflect the growing attention to the areas of conflict and consistency. Both are
important, and both have to be a part of the mindset. Learning together in a team
allows the team to begin to see the way it constructs collective and personal
meaning, but only if it maintains learning about its learning as a part of the cycle
of analysis.

Argyris' (1990) insight is helpful here. He argued that team actions can be
usefully described through single- or double-loop learning. In single-loop learning
the team is engaged in a stimulus–response dynamic with the required change.
This approach sees change as having a single effect and is a politically expedient
route to take in response to mandatory reform inside a modern paradigm. It
implies that the response by the team is based on the effect determined by the
external source. In double-loop learning, the team response illustrates a more
socially accountable change, where the team recognizes the political requirement
to undertake a change, but will base the approach it takes on an internal analysis
of the likely contextual impact of that change (see Figure 7.1).

Questions raised by learning to learn in teams include:

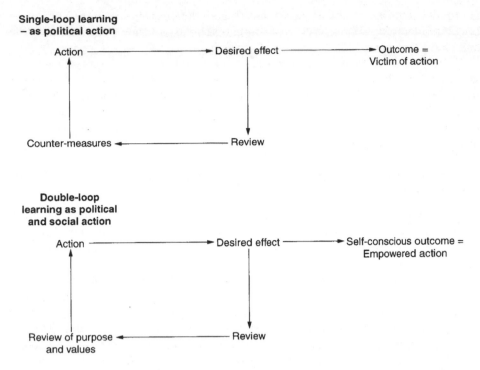

Figure 7.1 *Single- and double-loop learning*

- How do we promote review time and feedback sessions?
- How do we maintain discussions over long timeframes and identify the patterns of success and failure?
- How do we avoid the creation of learning barriers as teams identify areas of difference?
- Does the use of different team structures reinforce the existing patterns of working or does it transform previous approaches?
- If you pursue further the answers you have gathered, what do you see as the major advantages and disadvantages you will encounter?
- Would you be willing to go further with the agendas for change that you and your school raise?

A NEED TO CREATE SPACE

I sometimes can't hear myself think; in fact, come to think of it, I almost always can't hear myself think!
   (Headteacher to her staff in a staff meeting)

This challenge involves the creation of time to allow differences that have been identified to be examined and debated. It requires choices to be made and justified by asking, 'What can we lose from our present working activity so that other time is created to do more important things?' It also implies that the school, if it is to become a learning school, will have to change its use of time to accommodate a sustained conversation.

Creating the time and the space to understand better the perspectives being advanced by members of the team and by the wider community on the meaning of a learning school will be costly and will not necessarily show immediate outcome results, but it is a necessary activity because if we do not do it, we remain time-locked and our school and our school teams cease to have the opportunity to learn. Instead they will continue to be what many already believe they are, implementors of someone else's plan.

There are two points to be made about the development of living with this complex picture:

- First, addressing such issues takes up mental energy on a personal and at a team level. There needs to be processing time, and there needs to be opportunity for formal and informal space to reflect and reconstruct a view of the emerging change and how it feels in school.
- Second, the open-ended issues (often the riskiest ones), which are presently being cut out of organizations in favour of sticking to duties that relate to the day-to-day tasks of the job, imply that staff roles and responsibilities will need rethinking in order to create some space. It is not sufficient to make 'development commitment time' another managerial duty of the teaching staff on top of all the other duties, as this will invariably be a contrived form of collegiality (Hargreaves, 1994) lending to unintended consequences of avoidance and superficiality suggested earlier (Hargreaves, 1994). If the classroom exceeding role (MacGilchrist *et al.*, 1995) is to be realized and properly acknowledged as an important feature of school organizational life, then it has to have some real space for thinking and learning into the future.

SEEING AND DOING SCHOOLS DIFFERENTLY

In this book I have suggested that schools might fruitfully pursue other, more appropriate approaches that describe a school holistically, rather than taking the organization to pieces, analysing each part independently and then trying to put it all back together to see the whole.

The more holistic approach demands a different way of seeing schools, a different way of thinking and a different way of living and working with schools. It associates a series of different metaphors and meaning to school improvement. In particular this involves:

- Recognizing the delicacy of school as a culture;
- Seeing the interrelated nature of strategies which will affect that culture, and patterns of working that are structured through actions;
- Acknowledging that much of what school does concerns the journey and not a particular event;
- Recognizing the initiating point of a lifelong experience which is both personal, social and political;

- Acknowledging that we are embarked upon a creative, rather than a received experience;
- Acknowledging that we are embarked upon a risky and challenging experience;
- Realizing that this experience is an expression of freedom and democratic trust in people;
- Accepting a commitment to become 'a part of', rather than 'apart from' the social, cultural and economic world.

I have argued that our ways of thinking about this are at a transformational point. I would see the next century as being the time of breaking away from the past ways, in which control and order were paramount, into a new societal order in which previously established boundaries are breaking or broken down and new integrated norms emerge (Fukuyama, 1999). This action is driven by learning that takes hold at the political, economic, social and technical levels on the local and the global stage. These facts of contemporary life fuse new ways of conceptualizing the meaning of our schools, because schools are a part of this climate of redefinition and as participants in shaping it they too are shaped by it. Schools will therefore increasingly be seen as artefacts of a bygone age unless there is a concerted effort to challenge the present developmental discourses and pitch the thinking into the future agenda, the future learning the school will facilitate.

In this book I have outlined just a few of the conceptual issues and tools that are being used with schools and teachers today in order to facilitate thinking about the learning schools of tomorrow. These tools are no more than that; the critical thing about their use is the thoughts that they trigger about the substance, content and focus of schooling and school 'facilitating the technology of flowing ideas' (Druckner, 1993).

Many reformists, Druckner included, argue that technology will be the most important transformational feature of school change. I would challenge this notion. To see improvement in this technical way is to perpetuate the myth that we can solve our persistent problems through mechanistic approaches. I maintain that people are the most important transformational tool, and the way that people tolerate a situation or challenge it makes the difference to a school's role as a powerful place of learning. Technology will, if used in ways that service human social objectives, assist in getting us there, but it cannot do it alone and we should not be deluded into thinking that it can. Changing times promote new ways of doing old things; they do not necessarily mean that we will learn and do new things as a result of new times. We have a choice about this, and we exercise it by action or by default.

THE LEARNING SCHOOL

This new thinking on schools brings us to a reconsideration of the purpose of the school. This has a twofold meaning for me: first, it has to address individual learning needs and, second it, has to address the needs of the people. These are complementary and interwoven needs. They demand that the learner is provided with learning support of the very highest quality and is engaged in that learning within communities of learners which are wider than the present system allows. Schools therefore need to widen the scope of opportunities for learners of all ages, and they have to become learning places, rather than places of control and maintenance of the present system. Schools play the role of transforming the present into the future, and they are therefore centrally significant in the creation of a new agenda of learning that can challenge the old ways, which continue to fail so many of those learners who pass through school.

The 'learning school' will function as a complex adaptive system (Levin, 1993) and it has to be 'self-aware' to do this. Currently, schools face innumerable difficulties which cannot simply be captured and applied by some catch-all super-method of intervention. What we experience daily in school are the messes of problems swirling together, covering technical, social, political, environmental, organizational and individual dimensions. Our understanding of an approach to the task of supporting schools in dealing with change would be helped vastly if schools were not sold the myth that there are solutions to these problems 'out there on the shelves'. It would be better if schools began to operate with the conceptualization that the swirl is accepted as a normal part of school and social reality, just as the order reflects another part of school reality, and that we can live with this complexity.

To accommodate this mindset we need to develop new ways of conceptualizing our work and to work on the development of a set of rich methodological approaches which can frequently draw us into the sort of intervention approach we need to take in order to respond suitably to the problem situations that we find ourselves in, knowing that this task will often be messy and complex. Our involvement with schools in the development of techniques to model problem situations suggests that these approaches enhance the understanding of intervention and deepen schools' own ability to question and to probe for meaning in their development beyond superficial change for change's sake. Such meaning implies a sense of purpose, and the techniques facilitate that search for purpose.

The approaches to intervention that we take raise the fear that we are dealing with only partial representations of reality, that we need the multiplicity of colleagues' insights to make better responses to given circumstances, together with an eye on the possibility of partial review being added from elsewhere through supported self-review and consultancy. School improvement activists must recognize school problems as integrated and systemic and improvement as an emancipatory developmental tool and not a damage-limitation exercise.

Being able to differentiate between intervention approaches and develop an interactive discourse with those teachers involved in the change effort enhances our ability to deal with the evolution of improvement techniques. What is appropriate on day one as a methodology might be totally inappropriate on day eighty-one, yet often we see the same approach applied time after time to different problems, with little or no understanding of why the technique is working or failing, or of what alternative approaches could be better applied.

The intervention analysis and mapping facilitate a change discourse that will not eliminate the 'random acts of kindness' (Hopkins, 1995) that permeate and often inhibit lasting improvement work. But they may at least begin to reduce some of the randomness through a more systematic and coherent conceptual approach.

KEY ISSUES AND IDEAS IN THIS CHAPTER

- Stepping into the future, we have to experiment in giving students considerably more voice in the learning process.
- Doing this is challenging, because it redefines the design of the school and requires the holding of a very different series of conversations about quality, partnership, co-operation and the conservation of success.
- I have revisited the questions asked at the start of the book concerned with expression and achievement of the new paradigm, and in response I have identified what schools might look at. As they respond to some of these challenges, they can begin to think about how they might respond further.
- The challenges concern:
  - A redefinition of control
  - The appropriate uses of power
  - The self-organizing of learning teams
  - An appreciation of multiplicity of view
  - A willingness to take risks
  - Learning to learn in groups
  - A need to create space
- These challenges will continue to occupy the emerging learning school for some considerable time to come, for they lie at the interface of the shift from one view of school to another.

Chapter 8

The Great Leap Forward

We shall not cease from exploration
And the end of all our exploring
Will be to arrive where we started
And know the place for the first time.
T.S.Eliot, 'Little Gidding'

Towards the end of his recent book *The Great Disruption* (1999), Francis Fukuyama revisits a central theme, asking

> 'Could the pattern [of ever increasing individualization within an isolating social system] experienced in the second half of the nineteenth century in Britain and America, or in Japan, repeat itself in the next generation or two?'
> (my edits in brackets)

He suggests not, and argues that many of the great turbulences in society have in fact run their course and that the slow process of re-norming has begun. As evidence of this Fukuyama cites the fact that rates of crime, divorce, and social and civil unrest have slowed substantially in the United States in the 1990s and that this will continue. In parallel with this macro-political process he suggests that the industrialized culture of ever-expanding individualism is also in decline as public recognition unfolds of the need, in a modern society, of a collective purpose expressed in values as well as in economic practices, which in turn determine social structures and outcomes which serve people and their human needs and not just those of the corporation. Fukuyama indicates, as many others have observed in the change literature, that these ideas need time to take root in the popular consciousness, but, give or take a generation or two, they will begin to become self-evident.

A central feature of the cultural shift from expanding individualism towards a renewed sense of social responsibility lies at the heart of my argument in this book. I have maintained that our schools are currently experiencing the interface of two powerful paradigms: the modern, which I believe is in decline, and the ecological, which is in ascendancy. I have described the paradigm in decline as one which seeks to fragment and individualize the experience of learning in the interests of the primary goal of economic prosperity and the idolization of self-fulfilment. In modern contexts self-fulfilment, as the essence of capitalism, validated particular ways of living and working, seeing and thinking, and I have suggested that the changing nature of our social world demands a different conceptualization of self-fulfilment, because while it may be a good, it should not be a god.

In the ascendancy is the paradigm of the improvement of schools as an emancipatory agenda for renewal and growth – the ecological paradigm. This paradigm takes seriously within the school the significant themes that are ever present in contemporary society and which continue to challenge us. These are social, political, spiritual, technological, economic, and environmental; they demand that all citizens participate and make their voices heard, rather than taking as given the inevitability of these themes. In redesigning schools we need to seek ways of fashioning a new agenda for learning, in order to develop the human understanding of how to proceed with a more meaningful and sustainable way of functioning across the community, the nation and the planet – not just because this might be a good thing, but because if we do not do it we will decline into a systemic approach that suits the few to the detriment of the many.

In this context, I think that the school becomes an increasingly relevant and necessary, rather than irrelevant, institution in our society, as it raises the importance of a sense of service to the wider community. As the late Cardinal Basil Hume recently observed:

> The paradox of true human happiness and real contentment is that they are ultimately found not by seeking them directly, but through seeking the good of others. We have allowed ourselves to be hoodwinked into thinking otherwise. We have created a culture of reward that devalues public service and elevates private gain, almost as if the former were parasitic on the latter. In fact the true wealth of any society is simply its people. The real wealth creators, therefore, are parents and teachers. Long term, everyone else depends on them.

This interface between service and self-fulfilment inevitably is at its most raw in those places which have been, and will remain, the points where society has a political grasp on its citizens – the major institutions. The school is one such place, and consequently the school either plays out the more demanding ascending agenda or conforms to the short-term and increasingly valueless argument in decline.

MAPPING THE SEARCH

We can map many features of the search for a new way of conceptualizing the role of schools by means of taking a walk through the territory of which we as educators find ourselves struggling to make sense. Let us do this by revisiting some of the central arguments of this book and using them as pointers on the journey, probing the thinking and providing us with some ways of seeing the modern improvement problem with a renewed clarity.

CRISIS: CHANGE AND CONFORMITY

First, I believe we can consider the present climate of educational reform as one of crisis. It is a crisis because people have lost confidence and self-belief in our schools and our school system, and as a result they take refuge in the tired and well-trodden ways of old mindsets, preferring to believe that it was somehow better in the past.

We know that we live in a period where old ways of working simply no longer hold firm, as we begin to recognize that our best efforts to remain fixed on those old ways, while they might make us feel temporarily safer, offer little long-term sanctuary. In examining this feature of our contemporary educational climate we therefore need to ask ourselves: what exactly are the barriers that educators place in front of themselves which stop schools from taking the great leap forward? How do the present organizational arrangements, to which we cling in fear of the unknown, inhibit us from making real change happen?

The search: tolerance and conflict

As this crisis deepens we search for different solutions to the question of how to educate the learner. In doing so we revisit some fundamental questions concerning educational purpose and function:

- What and who do we do schools for?
- What are the values that underpin our teaching and support our view of the learner?
- Do our schools serve a social function other than that of providing good employees?
- If so, how do we connect with this wider agenda in ways that people feel are compelling, meaningful and worthy of commitment and energy?

These questions will bring with them both conflict and confrontation inside schools and school systems, because many of the undeclared realities of the modern paradigm will be contradicted and shown to be shallow, technical and instrumental. Ask yourself as an individual, as a parent, as a teacher, as a team player, as a school, as a community: what do you really want to see students learning about in school?

The expedition and the exploration

Searches demand expeditions and explorations. Searches for truth will take us into places that we feel are threatening and dangerous just as they will take us into places that are wonderful and inspiring. To undertake an expedition we have to become equipped with resources that will help us on the journey. I have suggested that we need to be both philosophers and mystics; we need to seek truth rationally and intuitively and to learn to accommodate both ways of seeing into our lives.

There are some essential items to facilitate this in the form of integrative approaches:

- We need allies to help us make progress and share the excitement and the tensions;
- We need to develop trust;
- We need security with each other to be able to take the necessary risks;
- We need inspiration from outside and we need to be able to draw inspiration from ourselves and our own context;
- We need the wisdom to judge what feels right and what does not;
- We need to know how to gather information to inform our feelings;
- We need to connect across boundaries and to develop the skills to hear each other and to find out how concerns and anxieties are enabling or inhibiting what we are doing.

In short, we need an attitude of mind that takes seriously the fact that learning is a risky, significant, life-changing process which is not exclusive to one's self but is an inherently social experience as well. In seeking responses to these questions, ask yourself what you draw upon to sustain and maintain your own learning, and how this might be shared with others in helping them to find their way on the journey.

Charting new frontiers, planning new journeys

Searches bring with them unexpected outcomes. In this book I have shown how some simple starting points have slowly developed and evolved into important learning-centred initiatives. To get there we had to move from the comfort and security of a tightly structured plan to a more fluid, emergent way of modelling change. This progress has the essence of map-making: the decision to act, followed by the practical activity of doing, serve as the peaks and valleys of the maps we create. The conversations we have and the doubts we share are the frontier points, as yet to be shaped and conceptualized into the image and language of the learner. Schools involved in some of the networks I have been attending over the recent years have been these new map-makers, searching for the right pathways to make their activity connect better with students as learners and with each other as leaders in their own expeditions. The have maintained a deliberate urgency of purpose whilst making good use of practical ways to monitor and map their changes, so that they could when necessary, stop and reflect on what aspects of learning and learners they were affecting and were affected by.

As we develop our schools I think we have to be in a position to cope with challenging and differing situations that arise out of nowhere yet offer considerable benefits for us if we move towards the development of the learning school. This is the process of living with complexity, knowing that entering into the search will make things more complex, not less, because it will open up a whole set of unknowns, with no predefined plans or formulas and no way of getting through the process other than by doing it. What we need to learn, as this search continues, is how to keep people connected so that they don't become lost. We need to understand that confusion is not always a negative state of mind and that absolute clarity often can be. We need to be able to support, collegially. This demands an emotional intelligence just as much as it demands a leadership and managerial intelligence. How can we maintain contact with other schools engaged in similar journeys, and how can the methods that we need to use to take advantage of emergent situations be encouraged, nurtured and embedded into the consciousness of the school?

STORYING THE SEARCH

All searches and all expeditions have their stories, their tales of mystery and excitement and adventure. These are also a part of the improvement journey of schools as they change from schooling to learning. The legacy of the instrumental approach has been to move us into a way of documenting the growth we experience along the improvement journey as a series of mechanical steps, devoid of the passion and the panic of real life.

A learning school, transformed from individualized to shared experience, will learn to enjoy the immediate experience of the journey and will convey that story successfully to others, so that they too find ways of comprehending their own learning and can see it happening in others. It will recognize the ongoing nature of the search and the importance of the journey, not just the security sought in reaching the desired destination. This is the legacy of the learning school, living as it does with the complexity of our times – dealing with the challenges of the new and the rage of the old, and still being sensitive and able to nurture and develop in all learners the search for understanding, skill, meaning and purpose so that they can live fulfilling lives in a changing world.

I finish with a manifesto for learning schools, developed with teachers, children and parents as I have travelled and worked with them on their learning journeys.

- When people experience the empowerment of their own actions, and their own voice being heard within a group;
- when people realize that their actions make a difference and that they are ultimately responsible for those actions;
- when people build communities in response to challenges;
- when people take a risk and recognize the creative possibilities that emerge from disequilibrium;
- when people foster self-reference and self-validation rather than depending on the external validation of an unseeing or unhearing other;
- when people collectively challenge and contest meaning and beliefs;
- when people become involved in decision processing;
- when people work with the flow;
- when people talk the future and look for trends to inform their discourse in the present;
- when people nurture democracy;

- when people encourage pluralism;
- when people believe in the possibility of each other;
- when the school of today initiates thinking in these new domains that are rising before it, treading between two powerful ways of seeing the world and choosing a route that better serves their collective and personal needs;

then that school is becoming the school of tomorrow, it will learn to live with complexity and it will be a learning school taking the search into a learning system further.

References

Ainscow, M. and Southworth, G. (1996) 'Working with schools: puzzles and problems in process consultancy and school improvement', American Education Research Association paper. New York.

Ainscow, M., Hargreaves, D.H., Hopkins, D., Balshaw, M., and Black-Hawkins, K. (1994) *Mapping Change in Schools: The Cambridge Manual of Research Techniques*. Cambridge: University of Cambridge Institute of Education.

Apple, M. W. (1983) 'Work, class and teaching', in S. Walker and L. Barton (eds), *Gender, Class and Education*. London: Falmer Press.

Apple, M.W. (1998) 'How the conservative restoration is justified: leadership and subordination in educational policy', *International Journal of Leadership in Education*, **1**(1), 3–17.

Argyris, C. (1990) *Overcoming Organisational Defences*.Needham Heights: Allyn and Bacon.

Argyris, C. and Schon, D. (1978) *Organisational Learning : A Theory of Action Perspective*. Reading, MA: Addison Wesley.

Badaracco, J.L. and Ellsworth, R. (1989) *Leadership and the Quest for Integrity*.Boston: Harvard Business School Press.

Bateson, G. (1979) *Steps into an Ecology Of Mind*. New York: Ballantine.

Baudrillard, J. (1994) *The Illusion of the End*. Cambridge: Polity Press.

Bayliss, S. (1999) *Opening Minds: Education for the 21st Century*. London: Royal Society of Arts publications.

Beare, H. (1997) 'Designing a break-the-mould school for the future'. Paper presented at the virtual conference of the Australian Council for Educational Administration.

Beare, H., Slaughter, R. and Jones, B. (1994) *Education for the Twenty-first Century*. London: Routledge.

Binney, G. and Williams, C. (1995) *Leaning Into The Future – Changing The Way People Change Organisations*. London: Nicholas Brearley Publishing.

Blase, J. and Anderson, G. (1995) *The Micropolitics of Educational Leadership*. London: Cassell.

Bohm, D. (1995) *Wholeness and the Implicate Order*. London: Routledge.

Bohm, D (1996) *On Dialogue*. London: Routledge.

Boyle, B. and Clarke, P. (1998) *The Headteacher as Effective Leader*. Buckingham: Ashgate.

Brown, L. (1981) *Building a Sustainable Society*. New York: Norton.

Caldwell, B.J. and Hayward, D.K. (1998) *The Future of Schools: Lessons from the Reform of Public Education*. London: Falmer Press.

Campbell, S. (1996) *From Chaos to Confidence*. New York: Simon and Schuster.

Campbell, J. (1988) *The Hero with a Thousand Faces*. London: Fontana.

Capra, F. (1996) *The Web of Life*. London: HarperCollins.

Carnegie Corporation (1983) *Education and Economic Progress: Towards a National Economic Policy*. New York: Carnegie Corporation.

Carr, W. and Kemmis, S. (1986). *Becoming Critical: Education, Knowledge and Action Research*. London: Falmer Press.

Carroll, L. (1998) *Through the Looking Glass*. London: Macmillan Children's Books.

Checkland, P. and Scholes, J. (1990) *Soft Systems Methodology in Action*. Chichester: Wiley.

Clark, D., Lotto, S. and Astuto, T. (1984). 'Effective schools and school improvement: a comparative analysis of two lines of inquiry', *Educational Administration Quarterly*, **20** (3).

Clarke, P. (1996) 'The nature and mechanisms of primary school change'. Unpublished PhD thesis, University of Manchester.

Clarke, P. (writing as Sam Stotley) (1999a) 'An edited extract from the teleconferenced speech to the Community of Learners Special Conference', *Improving Schools* **2**(2), 31–3.

Clarke, P. (1999b) 'Improving school intervention approaches: facilitative activity for learning schools'. *Evaluation and Research in Education*, **13**(1), 32–45.

Clarke, P. and Christie, T. (1995) 'Assessment led curriculum development in action: a study of seven primary schools responses to statutory requirements', *International Journal of Education Management*, **9**(4), 19–27.

Clarke, P and Christie, T. (1996) 'Trialling agreement: a discourse for a change', *British Journal of Curriculum and Assessment*, **6**(2), 12–18.

Clarke P. and Christie, T. (1997) 'Mapping changes in primary schools – what are we doing and where are we going?' *School Effectiveness and School Improvement*, **7** (3).

Clarke, P. (forthcoming) 'Target setting and the illusion of certainty?, in P. Clarke, *Target Setting: What's In It for Schools?* London: Falmer Press.

Clarke, P., Reed, J. and Lodge, C. (1998). *Reconceptualising School Improvement: From Instrumentalism to Sustainability*. Proceedings, International Congress for School Effectiveness and Improvement 1998. CD ROM, University of Manchester.

Claxton, G. (1997) *Hare Brain, Tortoise Mind: Why Intelligence Increases When You Think Less*. London: Fourth Estate.

Codding, J. (1997) 'Designing highly effective programs for successful schools'. Keynote presentation at the Successful Schools Conference, Melbourne, 3 June.

Commons, D.L. (Chair), (1985) *Who Will Teach Our Children? A Strategy for Improving California's Schools*. Sacramento, CA: California Commission on the Teaching Profession.

Connell, J., Kubisch, A., Schorr, L. and Wiess, C. (eds) (1995) *New Approaches to Evaluating Community Initiatives*. Aspen, CO: Aspen Institute.

Costa, A. and Garmston, B. (1994) *Cognitive coaching. A Foundation for Renaissance Schools*. Norwood, MA: Christopher Gordon Publishers.

Csikszentmihalyi, M. (1990) *Flow – The Psychology Of Optimal Experience*. New York: Harper and Row.

Csikszentmihalyi, M. (1993) *The Evolving Self: A Psychology for the Third Millennium*. New York: HarperCollins.

Csikszentmiahalyi, M. (1997) *Finding Flow – The Psychology of Engagement with Everyday Life*. New York: HarperCollins.

Cuban, L. (1995) 'The myth of failed school reform', *Education Week*, 1 November 1995.

Cuttance, P. (1994) 'Quality systems for the performance development cycle of schools'. Paper presented at the International Congress for School Effectiveness and School Improvement, Melbourne, January 1994.

Dalin, P. (1993) *Changing the School Culture*. London: Cassell.

Dalin, P. and Rust, V.D. (1994) *Towards Schooling for The Twenty-First Century*. London: Cassell.

References

Davies, D. (1987) *The Cosmic Blueprint. Order and Complexity at the Edge of Chaos.* London: Penguin Books.

De Gues, A. (1997) *The Living Company.* Cambridge, MA: Harvard Business School Press.

Department for Education and Employment [DfEE] (1997a) *Excellence in Schools.* London: Standards and Effectiveness Unit, DfEE.

Department for Education and Employment (1997b) *The Implementation of the National Literacy Strategy.* London: DfEE.

Department for Education and Employment (1998) *Meeting the Challenge of Change.* London: DfEE.

Dreyfus, H. and Rabinow, P. (1983) *Michel Foucault: Beyond Structuralism and Hermeneutics.* New York: Harvester Press.

Druckner, P. (1993) *Post-Capitalist Society.* Oxford: Butterworth-Heinemann.

Eliot, T.S. (1963) *Collected Poems.* London: Faber and Faber.

Evans, R. (1996) *The Human Side of School Change: Reform, Resistance and the Real-Life Problems of Innovation.* San Francisco: Jossey Bass.

Fairclough, N. (1989) *Language and Power.* Language in Social Life Series. London: Longman.

Fielding, M. (1996). 'Mapping change in schools: developing a new methodology'. Paper presented at American Education Research Association, New York, April.

Freire, P. (1974) *Education for Critical Consciousness.* New York: Continuum.

Fukuyama, F. (1999) *The Great Disruption.* London: Profile Books.

Fullan, M. (1991) *The New Meaning of Educational Change.* London: Cassell.

Fullan, M. (1993) *Change Forces: Probing the Depths of Educational Reform.* New York: Falmer Press.

Fullan, M. (1999) *Change Forces: The Sequel.* London: Falmer Press.

Fullan, M. and Hargreaves, A. (1992) *What's Worth Fighting For in Your School?* Buckingham: Open University Press.

Garmston, R. and Wellman, B. (1995) 'Adaptive schools in a quantum universe', *Educational Leadership,* **52**(7), 6–12.

Gleick, J. (1987) *Chaos.* London: Sphere Books.

Goleman, D. (1996). *Emotional Intelligence. Why It Can Matter More Than IQ.* London: Bloomsbury.

Goodwin, B. (1994) *How The Leopard Changed Its Spots.* New York: Scribner.

Gray, J., Hopkins, D., Reynolds, D., Wilcox, B., Farrell, S. and Jesson, D. (1999) *Improving Schools: Performance and Potential.* Buckingham: Open University Press.

Grundy, S. (1987) *Curriculum: Product or Praxis.* London: Falmer Press.

Guba, E. and Lincoln, Y. (1989) *Fourth Generation Evaluation.* London: Sage.

Hage, J. and Powers, C. (1992) *Post Industrial Lives – Roles and Relationships in the 21st Century.* London: Sage Publications.

Handy, C. (1998) 'Labour market flexibility: business strategies', in *The Hungry Spirit: Beyond Capitalism: A Quest for Purpose in the Modern World.* London: Arrow.

Hargreaves, A. (1994) *Changing Teachers, Changing Times – Teachers' Work and Culture in the Postmodern Age.* London: Cassell.

Hargreaves, D.H. (1995) 'School Culture, School Effectiveness and School Improvement', *School Effectiveness and School Improvement,* **6**(1).

Hargreaves, D.H. (1999) 'The knowledge creating school'. *British Journal of Educational Studies,* **47**(2), June, 122–44.

Hart, D. (1997) cited in *The Guardian,* 21 August 1997, p.1.

Hitchins, D. (1992) *Putting Systems to Work.* Chichester: Wiley.

Hochschild, A.R. (1983) *The Managed Heart. Commercialization of Human Feeling.* Berkeley: University of California Press.

Hopkins, D. (1995) 'Towards effective school improvement', *School Effectiveness and School Improvement* **6**(3), 265–74.

Hopkins, D., Ainscow, M. and West, M. (1994) *School Improvement in an Era of Change.* London: Cassell.

Huberman, M. (1993) 'Linking the researcher and practitioner communities for school improvement', *School Effectiveness and School Improvement*, **4**(1).

Huckle, J., and Sterling, S. (eds) (1996) *Education for Sustainability.* London: Earthscan.

Hume, B. (1999) Keynote speech to the Teacher Training Agency Conference, London, 18 March 1999.

Hustler, D., Cassidy, T. and Cuff, T. (eds) (1986) *Action Research in Classrooms and Schools.* London: Allen and Unwin.

Illich, I. and Verne, E. (1976) *Imprisoned in the Global Classroom.* London: Writers and Readers Publishing Co-operative.

Innes, M.M. (1955) *The Metamorphoses of Ovid.* London: Penguin Books.

Jackson, P., Raymond, L., Weatherill, L. and Fielding, M. (1998). 'Students as Researchers'. Symposium presentation at International Congress for School Effectiveness and Improvement, San Antonio, Texas.

Jefferson T. (1820) Letter to Charles Jarvis, 28 September 1820.

Joyce, B., Calhoun, E. and Hopkins, D. (1997) *Models of Learning – Tools for Teaching.* Buckingham: Open University Press.

Kegan, R. (1982) *The Evolving Self.* Harvard: Harvard University Press.

Kegan, R. (1995) *In Over Our Heads: The Mental Demands of Modern Life.* Harvard: Harvard University Press.

Khan, S.A. (1996) 'A vision of a twenty-first century learning centre', in Huckle and Sterling, 1996.

Knudsen, E. (1999) *Signs of Life.* Todmorden: Valence Films Ltd.

Kosko, B. (1993) *Fuzzy thinking.* London: HarperCollins.

Kruse, S.D. and Louis, K.S. (1993) 'An emerging framework for analyzing school-based professional community'. Paper presented at the annual meeting of the American Education Research Association, Atlanta, GA.

Kuhn, T. (1970) *The Structure of Scientific Revolutions.* 2nd edition. Chicago: University of Chicago Press.

'Labour market flexibility: Business strategies, London', cited in Handy, 1998, p. 70.

Leithwood, K. (1992) 'What have we learned and where do we go from here?' *School Improvement and School Effectiveness*, **3**(2), 173–84.

Leithwood, K. (1994) 'Leadership for school restructuring'. Address to the International Congress for School Effectiveness and School Improvement, Melbourne, January 1994.

Leithwood, K. and Louis, K. (1998) *Organizational Learning in Schools. Contexts of Learning.* Rotterdam: Swets and Zeitlinger.

Levin, R. (1993) *Complexity: Life at the Edge of Chaos.* London: Phoenix.

Louis, K. (1994) 'Beyond "Managed Change". Rethinking how schools improve,' *School Effectiveness and School Improvement*, **5**(1), 2–24.

Louis, K. and Marks, H. (1996) 'Does professional community affect the classroom?' Paper presented at the American Education Research Association, New York, 25 March.

Louis, K. and Miles, M. (1991) *Improving the Urban High School.* London: Cassell.

MacGilchrist, B., Mortimore, P., Savage, J. and Beresford , C. (1995) *Planning Matters. The Impact of Development Planning in Primary Schools.* London: Paul Chapman.

Miles, M. (1993) 'Forty Years' change in schools: Some personal reflections', *Educational Administration Quarterly*, **24**(2), 213–48.

Miles, M. and Huberman, M. (1994) *Qualitative Data Analysis: An Expanded Sourcebook*. 2nd edition. London: Sage.

Mintzberg, H. (1989) 'Planning on the left side, managing on the right', in H. Mintzberg, *Mintzberg on Management*. New York: Free Press.

Mintzberg, H. (1994) *The Rise and Fall of Strategic Planning*. New York: Prentice Hall.

Mkhatshwa, S. (1999) 'Improving schools in South Africa', in Townsend, Clarke and Ainscow, 1999.

Morgan, G. (1986) *Images of organisation*. London: Sage.

Mulgan, G. (1998) *Connexity*. London: Vintage.

Myers, K. (1995) *School Improvement in Practice*. London: Falmer Press.

National Commission on Excellence in Education (1983) *A Nation at Risk: The Imperative for Educational Reform*. Washington, DC: US Government Printing Office.

Neill, A.S. (1992) *The New Summerhill*. London: Penguin Books.

Newmann, F.M. and Wehlage, G.G. (1995) *Successful School Restructuring: A Report to the Public and Educators by the Center on Organizational Restructuring of Schools*. Madison, WI: Wisconsin Center for Educational Research.

Nias, J., Southworth, G. and Yeomans, R. (1989) *Staff Relationships in the Primary School*. London: Cassell.

Oatley, K. (1992) *Best Laid Plans. The Psychology of Emotions*. Cambridge: Cambridge University Press.

Olds, L. (1992) *Metaphors of Interrelatedness*. New York: SUNY Press.

Orr, D. (1994) *Earth in Mind : On Education, Environment, and the Human Prospect*. New York: Island Press.

Porritt, J. (1996) Introduction, in Huckle and Sterling, 1996.

Pring, R. (1998) Keynote presentation given at the Human Scale Education Conference, Oxford University, September.

Rabin, D. (1998) 'Seeking truth', *Resurgence*, 188 (May/June), 23.

Rifkin, J. (1995) *The End of Work: The Decline of the Global Labour Force and the Dawn of the Post-modern Era*. New York: Putnam Books.

Rilke, R. M. (1986) *The Complete French Poems of Rainer Maria Rilke*, edited by A. Poulin Jr. Graywolf Press.

Rio Declaration on Environment and Development (1992) 'Society is in the midst of crisis and heading for an ecological abyss'. Introduction.
Available from < http://sedac.ciesin.org/pidb/#searching >

Sackney, L. (1999) 'Learning Communities'. Paper presented at International Congress for School Effectiveness and Improvement, 5 January 1999. San Antonio, TX.

Sammons, P., Hillman, J. and Mortimore, P. (1995) *Key Characteristics of Effective Schools: A Review of School Effectiveness Research*. London: OFSTED.

Sankara, T. (1995) 'Who killed the Lion King?' Speech at the Congress of African States. *New Internationalist*, 268, 22–4.

Sarason, S. (1990) *The Predictable Failure of School Reform*. San Franciso: Jossey-Bass.

Saul, J.R. (1997) *The Unconscious Civilization*. London: Penguin Books.

Schein, E.H. (1992) *Organisational Culture and Leadership*. 2nd edition. San Francisco: Jossey Bass.

Schlechty, P. (1990) *Schools for the Twenty-First Century : Leadership Imperatives for Educational Reform*. San Francisco: Jossey-Bass.

Schwab, J. (1964) 'Structure of the disciplines: meanings and significances', in G.W. Ford and L. Pugno, *The Structure of Knowledge and the Curriculum*. Chicago: Rand McNally.

Senge, P. (1990) *The Fifth Discipline*. London: Century Business.

Senge, P. , Kleiner, A., Roberts, C. and Smith, B. (1994) *The Fifth Discipline Fieldbook*. London: Nicholas Brearley Publishing.

Sergiovanni, T. (1992) *Moral Leadership: Getting to the Heart of School Improvement*. San Francisco: Jossey-Bass.

Slaughter, R. (1994) *From Fatalism to Foresight – Educating for the Early 21st Century*. Melbourne: Australian Council for Educational Administration.

Smith, M. (1996) 'Research-based school reform: the Clinton Administration's agenda', in E. Hanushek and D. Jorgensen (eds), *Improving America's Schools: The Role of Incentives*. Washington DC: National Academy Press.

Smith, M., Clarke, P. and Chalmers, I. (1996) 'Improving standards in schools'. Briefing document, internal resources, Tameside LEA.

Spring, G. (1997) 'Education reform in Victoria, 1992–96: schools of the future'. Paper presented at the 10th International Congress for School Effectiveness and Improvement, Memphis, TN, January.

Starratt, R.S. (1995) *The Drama of Leadership*. London: Falmer Press.

Steinberg, L. (1996) *Beyond the Classroom: Why School Reform has Failed and What Parents Need to Do*. New York: Simon and Schuster.

Stoll, L., McBeath, J. and Robertson, P. (1999) 'The change equation: a study of Scottish Schools' capacity for improvement and effectiveness.' Paper presented as part of the symposium Exploring Capacity for Improvement in Schools: Perspectives from Four Countries, at American Education Research Association, Montreal. San Antonio, TX.

Stoll, L. and Fink, D. (1996) *Changing Our Schools*. Buckingham: Open University Press.

Stoll, L. and Myers, K. (1998) *No Quick Fixes*. London: Falmer.

Summers, A. and Johnson, A. W. (1996) 'The Effects of school-based management plans', in Hanushek and Jorgenson, 1996.

Thompson, J. (1999) 'The Green Paper: a magical solution to school improvement?', *Improving Schools*, **2**(2), 35–7.

Tilby, A. (1989) *Let There Be Light*. London: Darton, Longman and Todd.

Todnem, G. and Warner, M. (1995) 'Using assessment data in SIP decision making', *Journal of Staff Development*, **16**(2), 33–8, Spring.

Toffler, A. (1970) *Future Shock*. London: Pan Books.

Townsend, T. (1994) *Effective Schooling for the Community*. London and New York: Routledge.

Townsend, T. (1995) 'Schools of the future: a case study in systemic educational development'. Paper presented at the 8th International Congress for School Effectiveness and Improvement, Norrköping, January.

Townsend, T., Clarke, P. and Ainscow, M. (eds) (1999) *Third Millennium Schools: A World of Difference in Effectiveness and Improvement*. Rotterdam: Swets and Zeitlinger.

Troman, G. (1989) 'Testing tensions: the politics of educational assessment', *British Educational Research Journal*, **15**(3), 279–95.

UNESCO (1996) Learning: *The Treasure Within*. Report to UNESCO of the International Commission on Education for the Twenty-first Century, chaired by Jacques Delors. Paris: UNESCO.

Weiss, C. (1995) 'The four I's of school reform: How Interests, Ideology, Information, and Institution affect teachers and principals', *Harvard Educational Review*, **65**(4), 571–92, Winter.

Wheatley, M. (1994) *Leadership and the New Science*. San Francisco: Berrett-Koehler.

White, T.H. (1987) *The Once and Future King*, quoted in P.J. Palmer (1998) *The Courage to Teach: Exploring the Inner Landscape of a Teacher's Life*. San Francisco: Jossey-Bass, 1998.

References

Wilson, E.O. (1999) *Conscilience. The Unity of Knowledge.* London: Vintage Books.

Wolstenholme, E. (1990) *System Enquiry: A Systems Dynamics Approach.* Chichester: Wiley.

Woodhead, C. (1998), quoted in *The Times Educational Supplement* Analysis, p. 28, 26 September 1998.

Young, D.N., Bishop of Ripon (1994) *Parliamentary Debates*, House of Lords, 2 February.

Zohar, D. and Marshall, I. (1993) *The Quantum Society.* London: Bloomsbury.

Index

Index